Air Fryer Cookbook For Beginners On a Budget

350 Days of Quick, Easy and Healthy Recipes.
Amaze Your Guests With Your Delicious Recipes.

Breakfast and Brunch - Lunch and Dinner
Snacks and Appetizer - Desserts
Beef, Pork and Lamb - Fish and Sea Food
Poultry Recipes

Luisa Morris

Table of Contents
Breakfast and Brunch

Table of Contents
Lunch and Dinner

Table of Contents
Snack and Appetizers

Table of Contents
Desserts

Table of Contents
Beef, Pork and Lamb

Table of Contents
Fish and Sea Food

Table of Contents
Poultry Recipes

Breakfast and Brunch

Chorizo Risotto

Servings: 4
Cooking Time: 1 Hour 20 Minutes

Ingredients:

- ¼ cup milk
- ½ cup flour
- 4 oz. breadcrumbs
- 4 oz. chorizo, finely sliced
- 1 serving mushroom risotto rice
- 1 egg
- Sea salt to taste

Directions:

1. In a bowl, combine the mushroom risotto rice with the risotto and salt before refrigerating to cool.
2. Set your Air Fryer at 390°F and leave to warm for 5 minutes.
3. Use your hands to form 2 tablespoonfuls of risotto into a rice ball. Repeat until you have used up all the risotto. Roll each ball in the flour.
4. Crack the egg into a bowl and mix with the milk using a whisk. Coat each rice ball in the egg-milk mixture, and then in breadcrumbs.
5. Space the rice balls out in the baking dish of the Air Fryer. Bake for 20 minutes, ensuring they develop a crispy golden-brown crust.
6. Serve warm with a side of fresh vegetables and salad if desired.

Egg Yolks With Squid

Servings: 4
Cooking Time: 20 Minutes

Ingredients:

- ½ cup self-rising flour
- 14 ounces squid flower, cleaned and pat dried
- Salt and freshly ground black pepper
- 1 tablespoon olive oil
- 2 tablespoons butter
- 2 green chilies, seeded and chopped
- 2 curry leaves stalks
- 4 raw salted egg yolks
- ½ cup chicken broth
- 2 tablespoons evaporated milk
- 1 tablespoon sugar

Directions:

1. Set the temperature of Air Fryer to 355 degrees F. Grease an Air Fryer pan.
2. In a shallow dish, add the flour.
3. Sprinkle the squid flower evenly with salt and black pepper.
4. Coat the squid evenly with flour and then shake off any excess flour.
5. Place the squid into the prepared pan in a single layer.
6. Air Fry for about 9 minutes.
7. Remove from the Air Fryer and set aside
8. Now, heat the oil and butter in a skillet over medium heat and sauté the chilies and curry leaves for about 3 minutes.
9. Add the egg yolks and cook for about 1 minute, stirring continuously.
10. Gradually, add the chicken broth and cook for about 3-5 minutes, stirring continuously.
11. Add in the milk and sugar and mix until well combined.
12. Add the fried squid and toss to coat well.
13. Serve hot.

Parsnip Hash Browns

Servings: 2
Cooking Time: 20 Minutes

Ingredients:

- 3 eggs, beaten
- ½ tsp garlic powder
- ¼ tsp nutmeg
- 1 tbsp olive oil
- 1 cup flour
- Salt and pepper, to taste

Directions:

1. Heat olive oil in the air fryer at 390 F.
2. In a bowl, combine flour, eggs, parsnip, nutmeg, andgarlic powder. Season with salt and pepper.
3. Form patties out of the mixture.
4. Arrange in theAir Fryer and cook for minutes.

Very Berry Breakfast Puffs

Servings: 3
Cooking Time: 20 Minutes

Ingredients:

- 2 tbsp mashed strawberries
- 2 tbsp mashed raspberries
- ¼ tsp vanilla extract
- 2 cups cream cheese
- 1 tbsp honey

Directions:

1. Preheat the air fryer to 375 F. Divide the cream cheese between the dough sheets and spread it evenly. In a small bowl, combine the berries, honey and vanilla.
2. Divide the mixture between the pastry sheets. Pinch the ends of the sheets, to form puff. Place the puffs on a lined baking dish. Place the dish in the air fryer and cook for 15 minutes.

Crab Cheese Frittata

Servings: 2
Cooking Time: 14 Minutes

Ingredients:

- 5 eggs
- ¼ tsp fresh lemon juice
- 2 tbsp fresh mint, chopped
- 1/3 cup goat cheese, crumbled
- ¼ cup onion, minced
- ¼ tsp pepper
- ¼ tsp salt

Directions:

1. Preheat the air fryer to 325 F.
2. In a bowl, whisk eggs with pepper and salt. Add remaining ingredients and stir well.
3. Spray air fryer baking dish with cooking spray.
4. Pour egg mixture into the prepared dish and place in the Air Fryer and cook for 1minutes.
5. Serve and enjoy.

Artichoke Bowls

Servings: 4
Cooking Time: 20 Minutes

Ingredients:

- ½ pound artichokes, trimmed and chopped
- 2 zucchinis, sliced
- 4 spring onions, chopped
- 2 tomatoes, cut into quarters
- 4 eggs, whisked
- Cooking spray
- Salt and black pepper to the taste

Directions:

1. Grease a pan with cooking spray, and mix all the other ingredients inside.
2. Put the pan in the Air Fryer and cook at 350 degrees F for 20 minutes. Divide between plates and serve.

Coriander Sausages Muffins

Servings: 4
Cooking Time: 12 Minutes

Ingredients:

- 4 teaspoons coconut flour
- 1 tablespoon coconut cream
- 1 egg, beaten
- ½ teaspoon baking powder
- 6 oz sausage meat
- 1 teaspoon spring onions, chopped
- ½ teaspoon ground coriander
- 1 teaspoon sesame oil
- ½ teaspoon salt

Directions:

1. In the mixing bowl mix up coconut flour, coconut cream, egg, baking powder, minced onion, and ground coriander. Add salt and whisk the mixture until smooth. After this, add the sausage meat and stir the muffin batter.
2. Preheat the air fryer to 385F. Brush the muffin molds with sesame oil and pour the batter inside.
3. Place the rack in the air fryer basket. Put the muffins on a rack. Cook the meal for minutes.

Cheese and Chicken Sandwich

Servings: 1
Cooking Time: 15 Minutes

Ingredients:

- 1/3 cup chicken, cooked and shredded
- 2 mozzarella slices
- 1 hamburger bun
- ¼ cup cabbage, shredded
- 1 tsp. mayonnaise
- 2 tsp. butter
- 1 tsp. olive oil
- ½ tsp. balsamic vinegar
- 1/4 tsp. smoked paprika
- ¼ tsp. black pepper
- ¼ tsp. garlic powder
- Pinch of salt

Directions:

1. Pre-heat your Air Fryer at 370°F.
2. Apply some butter to the outside of the hamburger bun with a brush.
3. In a bowl, coat the chicken with the garlic powder, salt, pepper, and paprika.
4. In a separate bowl, stir together the mayonnaise, olive oil, cabbage, and balsamic vinegar to make coleslaw.
5. Slice the bun in two. Start building the sandwich, starting with the chicken, followed by the mozzarella, the coleslaw, and finally the top bun.
6. Transfer the sandwich to the fryer and cook for 5 – 7 minutes.

Chicken And Broccoli Quiche

Servings: 8
Cooking Time: 12 Minutes

Ingredients:

- 1 frozen ready-made pie crust
- 1 egg
- 1/3 cup cheddar cheese, grated
- ¼ cup boiled broccoli, chopped
- ¼ cup cooked chicken, chopped
- ½ tablespoon olive oil
- 3 tablespoons whipping cream
- Salt and black pepper, to taste

Directions:

1. Preheat the Air fryer to 390 o F and grease 2 small pie pans with olive oil.
2. Whisk egg with whipping cream, cheese, salt and black pepper in a bowl.
3. Cut 2 (5-inch) rounds from the pie crust and arrange in each pie pan.
4. Press in the bottom and sides gently and pour the egg mixture over pie crust.
5. Top evenly with chicken and broccoli and place the pie pans into an Air Fryer basket.
6. Cook for about 12 minutes and dish out to serve hot.

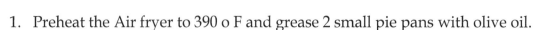

Cheese Pie

Servings: 4
Cooking Time: 16 Minutes

Ingredients:

- 8 eggs
- 1 1/2 cups heavy whipping cream
- 1 lb cheddar cheese, grated
- Pepper
- Salt

Directions:

1. Preheat the air fryer to 325 F.
2. In a bowl, whisk together cheese, eggs, whipping cream, pepper, and salt.
3. Spray air fryer baking dish with cooking spray.
4. Pour egg mixture into the prepared dish and place in the air fryer basket.
5. Cook for 16 minutes or until the egg is set.
6. Serve and enjoy.

Ground Pork Bake

Servings: 2
Cooking Time: 12 Minutes

Ingredients:

- 8 oz ground pork
- 1 tablespoon keto tomato sauce
- ½ teaspoon dried basil
- 1/3 cup Mozzarella, shredded
- ½ teaspoon butter, melted
- ¼ teaspoon dried oregano
- Cooking spray

Directions:

1. Preheat the air fryer to 365F. Then spray the air fryer basket with cooking spray.
2. In the mixing bowl mix up ground pork, marinara sauce, dried basil, oregano, butter, and Mozzarella.
3. Put the mixture in the air fryer basket and spread gently with the help of the spatula.
4. Cook the morning pizza for minutes.

Gourmet Cheesy Bread

Servings: 2
Cooking Time: 15 Minutes

Ingredients:

- 3 bread slices
- 2 tablespoons cheddar cheese
- 2 eggs, whites and yolks, separated
- 1 tablespoon chives
- 1 tablespoon olives
- 1 tablespoon mustard
- 1 tablespoon paprika

Directions:

1. Preheat the Air fryer to 355 o F and place the bread slices in a fryer basket.
2. Cook for about 5 minutes until toasted and dish out.
3. Whisk together egg whites in a bowl until soft peaks form.
4. Mix together cheese, egg yolks, mustard and paprika in another bowl until well combined.
5. Fold in egg whites gently and spread the mustard mixture over toasted bread slices.
6. Place in the Air fryer and cook for about 10 minutes.
7. Remove from the Air fryer and serve warm.

Feta Breakfast

Servings: 3
Cooking Time: 30 Minutes

Ingredients:

- pepper to taste
- 1 whole onion, chopped
- 2 tbsp parsley, chopped
- 1 egg yolk
- Olive oil for drizzling
- 5 sheets frozen filo pastry

Directions:

1. Cut each of the 5 filo sheets into three equal-sized strips. Cover the strips with oil. In a bowl, mix onion, pepper, feta, salt, egg yolk, and parsley.
2. Make triangles using the cut strips and add a little bit of the feta mixture on top of each triangle. Place in fryer's basket and cook for 3 minutes at 400 F. Serve with a drizzle of oil and green onions.

Buttery Scallops

Servings: 2
Cooking Time: 8 Minutes

Ingredients:

- 1 lb jumbo scallops
- 1 tbsp fresh lemon juice
- 2 tbsp butter, melted

Directions:

1. Preheat the air fryer to 400 F.
2. In a small bowl, mix together lemon juice and butter.
3. Brush scallops with lemon juice and butter mixture and place into the air fryer basket.
4. Cook scallops for minutes. Turn halfway through.
5. Again brush scallops with lemon butter mixture and cook for 4 minutes more. Turn half way through.
6. Serve and enjoy.

Yummy Breakfast Frittata

Servings: 2
Cooking Time: 14 Minutes

Ingredients:

- 6 cherry tomatoes, halved
- ½ cup Parmesan cheese, grated and divided
- 1 bacon slice, chopped
- 6 fresh mushrooms, sliced
- 3 eggs
- 1 tablespoon olive oil
- Salt and black pepper, to taste

Directions:

1. Preheat the Air fryer to 390 o F and grease a baking dish with olive oil.
2. Mix together tomatoes, bacon, mushrooms, salt and black pepper in a bowl.
3. Transfer into the baking dish and place in the Air fryer.
4. Cook for about 6 minutes and remove from the Air fryer.
5. Whisk together eggs and cheese in a bowl.
6. Pour the egg mixture evenly over bacon mixture and cook in the Air fryer for about 8 minutes.

French Frittata

Servings: 3
Cooking Time: 18 Minutes

Ingredients:

- 3 eggs
- 1 tablespoon heavy cream
- 1 teaspoon Herbs de Provence
- 1 teaspoon almond butter, softened
- 2 oz Provolone cheese, grated

Directions:

1. Crack the eggs in the bowl and add heavy cream. Whisk the liquid with the help of the hand whisker. Then add herbs de Provence and grated cheese.
2. Stir the egg liquid gently.
3. Preheat the Air Fryer to 365 F.
4. Then grease the air fryer basket with almond butter. Pour the egg liquid in the Air Fryer basket and cook it for minutes.
5. When the frittata is cooked, cool it to the room temperature and then cut into servings.

Chorizo Spanish Frittata

Servings: 2
Cooking Time: 12 Minutes

Ingredients:

- 1 large potato, boiled and cubed
- ½ cup frozen corn
- ½ cup feta cheese, crumbled
- 1 tbsp chopped parsley
- ½ chorizo, sliced
- 3 tbsp olive oil
- Salt and pepper, to taste

Directions:

1. Pour the olive oil into the air fryer and preheat it to 330 F.
2. Cook the chorizo until slightly browned. Beat the eggs with some salt and pepper in a bowl.
3. Stir in all of the remaining ingredients.
4. Pour the mixture into the air fryer, give it a stir, and cook for 6 minutes.

Vegetable Egg Souffle'

Servings: 4
Cooking Time: 20 Minutes

Ingredients:

- 4 large eggs
- 1 tsp onion powder
- 1 tsp garlic powder
- 1 tsp red pepper, crushed
- 1/2 cup broccoli florets, chopped
- 1/2 cup mushrooms, chopped

Directions:

1. Spray four ramekins with cooking spray and set aside.
2. In a bowl, whisk eggs with onion powder, garlic powder, and red pepper.
3. Add mushrooms and broccoli and stir well.
4. Pour egg mixture into the prepared ramekins and place ramekins into the air fryer basket.
5. Cook at 3 F for 15 minutes. Make sure souffle is cooked if souffle is not cooked then cook for 5 minutes more.
6. Serve and enjoy.

Eggplant And Zucchini Breakfast Mix

Servings: 4
Cooking Time: 45 Minutes

Ingredients:

- 8 ounces eggplant, sliced
- 8 ounces zucchini, sliced
- 8 ounces bell peppers, chopped
- 2 garlic cloves, minced
- 5 tablespoons olive oil
- 2 yellow onions, chopped
- 8 ounces tomatoes, cut into quarters
- Salt and black pepper to taste

Directions:

1. Heat up a pan that fits your air fryer with half of the oil over medium heat.
2. Add the eggplant, salt, and pepper. Stir, cook for 5 minutes, and then transfer to a bowl.
3. Heat up the pan with 1 tablespoon of oil, add the zucchini and the bell peppers, cook for 4 minutes, and then add to the eggplant pieces.
4. Heat up the pan with the remaining oil, add onions, stir, and sauté for 3 minutes.
5. Add the tomatoes, garlic, and if desired, more salt and pepper; stir.
6. Transfer the pan to your air fryer and cook at 300 degrees F for 30 minutes.
7. Divide mixture between plates and serve right away.

Spiced Pumpkin Bread

Servings: 4
Cooking Time: 25 Minutes

Ingredients:

- ¼ cup coconut flour
- 2 tablespoons stevia blend
- 1 teaspoon baking powder
- ¾ teaspoon pumpkin pie spice
- ¼ teaspoon ground cinnamon
- 1/8 teaspoon salt
- ¼ cup canned pumpkin
- 2 large eggs
- 2 tablespoons unsweetened almond milk
- 1 teaspoon vanilla extract

Directions:

1. In a bowl, mix together the flour, stevia, baking powder, spices, and salt.
2. In another large bowl, add the pumpkin, eggs, almond milk, and vanilla extract. Beat until well combined.
3. Then, add in the flour mixture and mix until just combined
4. Set the temperature of air fryer to 350 degrees F. Line a cake pan with a greased parchment paper.
5. Place the mixture evenly into the prepared pan.
6. Arrange the pan into an air fryer basket.
7. Air fry for about 25 minutes or until a toothpick inserted in the center comes out clean.
8. Remove the pans from air fryer and place onto a wire rack for about 5 minutes.
9. Carefully, take out the bread from pan and put onto a wire rack to cool for about 5-10 minutes before slicing.
10. Cut the bread into desired size slices and serve.

Breakfast Creamy Donuts

Servings: 8
Cooking Time: 18 Minutes

Ingredients:

- 4 tablespoons butter, softened and divided
- 2 large egg yolks
- 2¼ cups plain flour
- 1½ teaspoons baking powder
- 1 pinch baking soda
- 1/3 cup caster sugar
- 1 teaspoon cinnamon
- ½ cup sugar
- 1 teaspoon salt
- ½ cup sour cream

Directions:

1. Preheat the Air fryer to 355 o F.
2. Mix together sugar and butter in a bowl and beat until crumbly mixture is formed.
3. Whisk in the egg yolks and beat until well combined.
4. Sift together flour, baking powder, baking soda and salt in another bowl.
5. Add the flour mixture and sour cream to the sugar mixture.
6. Mix well to form a dough and refrigerate it.
7. Roll the dough into 2-inch thickness and cut the dough in half.
8. Coat both sides of the dough with the melted butter and transfer into the Air fryer.
9. Cook for about 8 minutes until golden brown and remove from the Air Fryer.
10. Sprinkle the donuts with the cinnamon and caster sugar to serve.

Air Fried Calzone

Servings: 4
Cooking Time: 20 Minutes

Ingredients:

- 4 oz cheddar cheese, grated
- 1 oz mozzarella cheese
- 1 oz bacon, diced
- 2 cups cooked and shredded turkey
- 1 egg, beaten
- 4 tbsp tomato paste
- 1 tsp basil
- 1 tsp oregano
- Salt and pepper, to taste

Directions:

1. Preheat the air fryer to 350 F. Divide the pizza dough into 4 equal pieces so you have the dough for 4 small pizza crusts.
2. Combine the tomato paste, basil, and oregano in a small bowl.
3. Brush the mixture onto the crusts, just make sure not to go all the way and avoid brushing near the edges on one half of each crust, place ½ turkey, and season the meat with some salt and pepper.
4. Top the meat with bacon.
5. Divide mozzarella and cheddar cheeses between pizzas.
6. Brush the edges with beaten egg.
7. Fold the crust and seal with a fork.
8. Cook for 10 minutes.

Oregano Chicken Casserole

Servings: 4
Cooking Time: 25 Minutes

Ingredients:

- ¼ cup almonds, chopped
- ½ cup almond milk
- 4 eggs, whisked
- 1 cup chicken meat, cooked and shredded
- ½ teaspoon oregano, dried
- Cooking spray
- Salt and black pepper to the taste

Directions:

1. In a bowl, mix the eggs with the rest of the ingredients except the cooking spray and whisk well.
2. Grease a baking pan with the cooking spray, pour the chicken mix into the pan, put the pan in the machine and cook the omelet at 350 degrees F for 25 minutes.
3. Divide between plates and serve for breakfast.

Toasted Cheese

Servings: 2
Cooking Time: 20 Minutes

Ingredients:

- 2 slices bread
- 4 oz cheese, grated
- Small amount of butter

Directions:

1. Grill the bread in the toaster.
2. Butter the toast and top with the grated cheese.
3. Set your Air Fryer to 0° F and allow to warm.
4. Put the toast slices inside the fryer and cook for 6 minutes.
5. Serve and enjoy!

Cheesy Sausage Sticks

Servings: 3
Cooking Time: 8 Minutes

Ingredients:

- 6 small pork sausages
- ½ cup almond flour
- ½ cup Mozzarella cheese, shredded
- 2 eggs, beaten
- 1 tablespoon mascarpone
- Cooking spray

Directions:

1. Pierce the hot dogs with wooden coffee sticks to get the sausages on the sticks". Then in the bowl mix up almond flour, Mozzarella cheese, and mascarpone.
2. Microwave the mixture for seconds or until you get a melted mixture.
3. Then stir the egg in the cheese mixture and whisk it until smooth.
4. Coat every sausage stick in the cheese mixture.
5. Then preheat the Air Fryer to 375 F.
6. Spray the Air Fryer basket with cooking spray.
7. Place the sausage stock in the Air Fryer and cook them for 4 minutes from each side or until they are light brown.

Turmeric Mozzarella Sticks

Servings: 2
Cooking Time: 7 Minutes

Ingredients:

- 4 oz Mozzarella
- 2 tablespoons coconut flakes
- 1 egg, beaten
- 1 teaspoon turmeric powder
- 1 tablespoon heavy cream
- ½ teaspoon ground black pepper
- Cooking spray

Directions:

1. Cut Mozzarella into 2 sticks. Then in the mixing bowl mix up heavy cream, egg, and ground black pepper.
2. Dip the cheese sticks in the liquid. After this, coat every cheese stick with coconut flakes.
3. Preheat the air fryer to 400 F.
4. Then spray the Air Fryer basket with cooking spray.
5. Put Mozzarella sticks in the Air Fryer and cook them for 7 minutes or until they are light brown.

Cheesy Mustard Toasts

Servings: 4
Cooking Time: 15 Minutes

Ingredients:

- 4 bread slices
- 2 tablespoons cheddar cheese, shredded
- 2 eggs, whites and yolks, separated
- 1 tablespoon mustard
- 1 tablespoon paprika

Directions:

1. Set the temperature of Air Fryer to 355 degrees F.
2. Place the bread slices in an Air Fryer basket.
3. Air Fry for about 5 minutes or until toasted.
4. Add the egg whites in a clean glass bowl and beat until they form soft peaks.
5. In another bowl, mix together the cheese, egg yolks, mustard, and paprika.
6. Gently, fold in the egg whites.
7. Spread the mustard mixture over the toasted bread slices.
8. Air Fry for about 10 minutes.
9. Serve warm!

Breakfast Omelet

Servings: 2
Cooking Time: 30 Minutes

Ingredients:

- 1 large onion, chopped
- 2 tbsp. cheddar cheese, grated
- 3 eggs
- ½ tsp. soy sauce
- Salt
- Pepper powder
- Cooking spray

Directions:

1. In a bowl, mix the salt, pepper powder, soy sauce and eggs with a whisk.
2. Take a small pan small enough to fit inside the Air Fryer and spritz with cooking spray. Spread the chopped onion across the bottom of the pan, then transfer the pan to the Fryer. Cook at 355° F for 6-7 minutes, ensuring the onions turn translucent.
3. Add the egg mixture on top of the onions, coating everything well. Add the cheese on top, then resume cooking for another 5 or 6 minutes.
4. Take care when taking the pan out of the fryer. Enjoy with some toasted bread.

Bacon Eggs

Servings: 2
Cooking Time: 5 Minutes

Ingredients:

- 2 eggs, hard-boiled, peeled
- 4 bacon slices
- ½ teaspoon avocado oil
- 1 teaspoon mustard

Directions:

1. Preheat the air fryer to 400 F.
2. Then sprinkle the air fryer basket with avocado oil and place the bacon slices inside.
3. Flatten them in one layer and cook for 2 minutes from each side.
4. After this, cool the bacon to the room temperature.
5. Wrap every egg into 2 bacon slices. Secure the eggs with toothpicks and place them in the Air Fryer.
6. Cook the wrapped eggs for minute at 400F.

Air Fryer Breakfast Bake

Servings: 2
Cooking Time: 25 Minutes

Ingredients:

- 4 eggs
- 1 slice whole grain bread, torn into pieces
- 1½ cups baby spinach
- 1/3 cup cheddar cheese, shredded
- ½ cup bell pepper, diced
- ½ teaspoon kosher salt
- 1 teaspoon hot sauce

Directions:

1. Preheat the Air Fryer to 250 o F and grease a 6-inch soufflé dish with nonstick cooking spray.
2. Whisk together eggs, salt and hot sauce in a bowl.
3. Dip the bread pieces, spinach, ¼ cup cheddar cheese and bell pepper in the whisked eggs.
4. Pour this mixture into prepared soufflé dish and sprinkle with remaining cheese.
5. Transfer into the Air Fryer basket and cook for about 2minutes.
6. Remove from the Air Fryer basket and let it rest for 10 minutes before serving.

Bread Cups Omelette

Servings: 4
Cooking Time: 25 Minutes

Ingredients:

- 5 eggs, beaten
- A pinch of salt
- ½ tsp thyme, dried
- 3 strips precooked bacon, chopped
- 2 tbsp heavy cream
- 4 Gouda cheese mini wedges, thin slices

Directions:

1. Preheat your Air Fryer 330 F.
2. Cut the tops off the rolls and remove the inside with yourfingers.
3. Line the rolls with a slice of cheese and press down, so the cheese conforms to the inside of the roll.
4. In a bowl, mix eggs with heavy cream, bacon, thyme, salt and pepper.
5. Stuff the rolls with the egg mixture.
6. Lay the rolls in your Air Fryer's cooking basket and bake for 8 to 1minutes or until the eggs become puffy and the roll shows a golden brown texture.

Tomatoes Casserole

Servings: 4
Cooking Time: 15 Minutes

Ingredients:

- 4 eggs, whisked
- 1 teaspoon olive oil
- 3 ounces Swiss chard, chopped
- 1 cup tomatoes, cubed
- Salt and black pepper to the taste

Directions:

1. In a bowl, mix the eggs with the rest of the ingredients except the oil and whisk well.
2. Grease a pan that fits the fryer with the oil, pour the swish chard mix and cook at 359 degrees F for minutes.
3. Divide between plates and serve for breakfast.

Tex-Mex Hash Browns

Servings: 4
Cooking Time: 30 Minutes

Ingredients:

- 1½ pounds potatoes, peeled, cut into 1-inch cubes and soaked
- 1 red bell pepper, seeded and cut into 1-inch pieces
- 1 small onion, cut into 1-inch pieces
- 1 jalapeno, seeded and cut into 1-inch rings
- 1 tablespoon olive oil
- ½ teaspoon taco seasoning mix
- ½ teaspoon ground cumin
- 1 pinch salt and ground black pepper, to taste

Directions:

1. Preheat the Air fryer to 330 o F and grease an Air fryer basket.
2. Coat the potatoes with olive oil and transfer into the Air fryer basket.
3. Cook for about 18 minutes and dish out in a bowl.
4. Mix together bell pepper, onion, and jalapeno in the bowl and season with taco seasoning mix, cumin, salt and black pepper.
5. Toss to coat well and combine with the potatoes.
6. Transfer the seasoned vegetables into the Air fryer basket and cook for about 12 minutes, stirring in between.
7. Dish out and serve immediately.

Coconut Muffins

Servings: 2
Cooking Time: 10 Minutes

Ingredients:

- 1/3 cup almond flour
- 2 tablespoons Erythritol
- ¼ teaspoon baking powder
- 1 teaspoon apple cider vinegar
- 1 tablespoon coconut milk
- 1 tablespoon coconut oil, softened
- 1 teaspoon ground cinnamon
- Cooking spray

Directions:

1. In the mixing bowl mix up almond flour. Erythritol, baking powder, and ground cinnamon.
2. Add apple cider vinegar, coconut milk, and coconut oil.
3. Stir the mixture until smooth.
4. Spray the muffin molds with cooking spray.
5. Scoop the muffin batter in the muffin molds.
6. Spray the surface of every muffin with the help of the spatula.
7. Preheat the Air Fryer to 365 F.
8. Insert the rack in the Air Fryer.
9. Place the muffins on the rack and cook them for minutes at 365 F.
10. Then cool the cooked muffins well and remove them from the molds.

Perfect Breakfast Frittata

Servings: 2
Cooking Time: 32 Minutes

Ingredients:

- 3 eggs
- 2 tbsp parmesan cheese, grated
- 2 tbsp sour cream
- 1/2 cup bell pepper, chopped
- 1/4 cup onion, chopped
- 1/2 tsp pepper
- 1/2 tsp salt

Directions:

1. Add eggs in a mixing bowl and whisk with remaining ingredients.
2. Spray Air Fryer baking dish with cooking spray.
3. Pour egg mixture into the prepared dish and place in the Air Fryer and cook at 365 F for 5 minutes.
4. Serve and enjoy

Mock Stir Fry

Servings: 4
Cooking Time: 25 Minutes

Ingredients:

- 2 carrots, sliced
- 1 red bell pepper, cut into strips
- 1 yellow bell pepper, cut into strips
- 1 cup snow peas
- 15 oz broccoli florets
- 1 scallion, sliced

Sauce:

- 3 tbsp soy sauce
- 2 tbsp oyster sauce
- 1 tbsp brown sugar
- 1 tsp sesame oil
- 1 tsp cornstarch
- 1 tsp sriracha
- 2 garlic cloves, minced
- 1 tbsp grated ginger
- 1 tbsp rice wine vinegar

Directions:

1. Preheat the Air Fryer to 370 F. Place the chicken, bell peppers, and carrot, in a bowl.
2. In another bowl, combine the sauce ingredients.
3. Coat the chicken mixture with the sauce.
4. Place on a lined baking sheet and cook for 5 minutes.
5. Add snow peas and broccoli and cook for an additional 8 to 10 minutes.
6. Serve garnished with scallion.

Peppers Rings

Servings: 2
Cooking Time: 11 Minutes

Ingredients:

- 1 large green bell pepper
- ½ cup ground beef
- 1 egg, beaten
- ½ teaspoon salt
- ½ teaspoon ground black pepper
- ½ teaspoon Italian seasonings
- 1 teaspoon coconut oil, melted

Directions:

1. Remove the seeds from the pepper and wash it.
2. Then cut the pepper into 2 rings.
3. In the bowl combine together egg, ground beef, salt, ground black pepper, and Italian seasonings.
4. Preheat the Air Fryer to 385 F.
5. Brush the Air Fryer basket with coconut oil.
6. Place the pepper rings in the Air Fryer and fill them with ground beef mixture.
7. Cook the meal at 385F for minutes.

Mascarpone Bites

Servings: 8
Cooking Time: 3 Minutes

Ingredients:

- 4 tablespoons cream cheese
- 4 teaspoons Erythritol
- ¼ teaspoon vanilla extract
- 1 tablespoon mascarpone
- 4 tablespoons coconut milk
- 4 tablespoons almond flour

Directions:

1. Mix up cream cheese with Erythritol, vanilla extract, and mascarpone.
2. Make the cheesecake balls (bites) and put them on the baking paper.
3. Refrigerate the cheesecake balls for -15 minutes.
4. Then preheat the Air Fryer to 300 F.
5. Dip the frozen bites in the coconut milk and coat in the almond flour.
6. Cook them in the Air Fryer for 3 minutes.

Parsley Omelet

Servings: 4
Cooking Time: 15 Minutes

Ingredients:

- 4 eggs, whisked
- 1 tablespoon parsley, chopped
- ½ teaspoons cheddar cheese, shredded
- 1 avocado, peeled, pitted and cubed
- Cooking spray

Directions:

1. In a bowl, mix all the ingredients except the cooking spray and whisk well.
2. Grease a baking pan that fits the Air Fryer with the cooking spray, pour the omelet mix, spread, introduce the pan in the machine and cook at 370 degrees F for minutes.
3. Serve for breakfast.

Stylish Ham Omelet

Servings: 2
Cooking Time: 30 Minutes

Ingredients:

- 4 small tomatoes, chopped
- 4 eggs
- 2 ham slices
- 1 onion, chopped
- 2 tablespoons cheddar cheese
- Salt and black pepper, to taste

Directions:

1. Preheat the Air Fryer to 390 o F and grease an Air Fryer pan.
2. Place the tomatoes in the Air Fryer pan and cook for about 10 minutes.
3. Heat a nonstick skillet on medium heat and add onion and ham.
4. Stir fry for about 5 minutes and transfer into the Air Fryer pan.
5. Whisk together eggs, salt and black pepper in a bowl and pour in the Air Fryer pan.
6. Set the Air Fryer to 335 o F and cook for about 15 minutes.
7. Dish out and serve warm.

Breakfast Sausage Casserole

Servings: 4
Cooking Time: 50 Minutes

Ingredients:

- 8 eggs, beaten
- 1 head chopped cauliflower
- 1 lb sausage, cooked and crumbled
- 2 cups heavy whipping cream
- 1 cup sharp cheddar cheese, grated

Directions:

1. Cook the sausage as usual.
2. In a large bowl, mix the sausage, heavy whipping cream, chopped cauliflower, cheese and eggs.
3. Pour into a greased casserole dish.
4. Cook for minutes at 350°F/175°C, or until firm.
5. Top with cheese and serve.

Mushroom Frittata

Servings: 1
Cooking Time: 13 Minutes

Ingredients:

- 1 cup egg whites
- 1 cup spinach, chopped
- 2 mushrooms, sliced
- 2 tbsp parmesan cheese, grated
- Salt

Directions:

1. Spray pan with cooking spray and heat over medium heat.
2. Add mushrooms and sauté for 3 minutes. Add spinach and cook for 1-2 minutes or untilwilted.
3. Transfer mushroom spinach mixture into the Air Fryer pan.
4. Whisk egg whites in a mixing bowl until frothy. Season with a pinch of salt.
5. Pour egg white mixture into the spinach and mushroom mixture and sprinkle with parmesan cheese.
6. Place pan in Air Fryer basket and cook frittata at 350 F for 8 minutes.
7. Slice and serve.

Banana Chia Seed Pudding

Servings: 1
Cooking Time: 1-2 Days

Ingredients:

- 1 can full-fat coconut milk
- 1 medium- or small-sized banana, ripe
- ½ tsp cinnamon
- 1 tsp vanilla extract
- ¼ cup chia seeds

Directions:

1. In a bowl, mash the banana until soft.
2. Add the remaining ingredients and mix until incorporated.
3. Cover and place in your refrigerator overnight.
4. Serve!

Nutty Zucchini Bread

Servings: 16
Cooking Time: 20 Minutes

Ingredients:

- 3 cups all-purpose flour
- 2 teaspoons baking powder
- 3 eggs
- 2 cups zucchini, grated
- 1 cup walnuts, chopped
- 1 tablespoon ground cinnamon
- 1 teaspoon salt
- 2¼ cups white sugar
- 1 cup vegetable oil
- 3 teaspoons vanilla extract

Directions:

1. Preheat the Air Fryer to 320 o F and grease two (8x4-inch) loaf pans.
2. Mix together the flour, baking powder, cinnamon and salt in a bowl.
3. Whisk together eggs with sugar, vanilla extract and vegetable oil in a bowl until combined.
4. Stir in the flour mixture and fold in the zucchini and walnuts.
5. Mix until combined and transfer the mixture into the prepared loaf pans.
6. Arrange the loaf pans in an Air Fryer basket and cook for about 20 minutes.
7. Remove from the Air Fryer and place onto a wire rack to cool.
8. Cut the bread into desired size slices and serve.

Coconut Eggs Mix

Servings: 4
Cooking Time: 8 Minutes

Ingredients:

- 1 tablespoon olive oil
- 1 and ½ cup coconut cream
- 8 eggs, whisked
- ½ cup mint, chopped
- Salt and black pepper to the taste

Directions:

1. In a bowl, mix the cream with salt, pepper, eggs and mint, whisk, pour into the Air Fryer greased with the oil, spread.
2. Cook at 350 degrees F for 8 minutes
3. Divide between plates and serve.

Mixed Peppers Hash

Servings: 4
Cooking Time: 20 Minutes

Ingredients:

- 1 red bell pepper, cut into strips
- 1 green bell pepper, cut into strips
- 1 orange bell pepper, cut into strips
- 4 eggs, whisked
- Salt and black pepper to the taste
- 2 tablespoons mozzarella, shredded
- Cooking spray

Directions:

1. In a bowl, mix the eggs with all the bell peppers, salt and pepper and toss.
2. Preheat the Air Fryer at 350 degrees F.
3. Grease it with cooking spray, pour the eggs mixture, spread well,sprinkle the mozzarella on top and cook for 20 minutes.
4. Divide between plates and serve for breakfast.

Butter Donuts

Servings: 4
Cooking Time: 10 Minutes

Ingredients:

- 1 cup almond flour
- 1 tablespoon flax meal
- 2 tablespoons Erythritol
- 2 eggs, beaten
- 1 teaspoon baking powder
- 1 teaspoon vanilla extract
- 1 teaspoon heavy cream
- 1 teaspoon butter, melted
- 1 tablespoon Psyllium husk powder

Directions:

1. Make the dough: mix up almond flour, flax meal, eggs, baking powder, vanilla extract, heavy cream, and butter.
2. Add Psyllium husk and knead the soft but non-sticky dough.
3. Then make the donuts balls and leave them for minutes in a warm place.
4. Preheat the Air Fryer to 355 F.
5. Line the Air Fryer basket with baking paper.
6. Put the donuts inside and cook them for 10 minutes or until they are light brown.
7. Then coat every donut in Erythritol.

Cherry Tomato Frittata

Servings: 2
Cooking Time: 10 Minutes

Ingredients:

- ½ of Italian sausage
- 4 cherry tomatoes, halved
- 3 eggs
- 1 tablespoon Parmesan cheese, shredded
- 1 teaspoon fresh parsley, chopped
- 1 tablespoon olive oil
- Salt and black pepper, to taste

Directions:

1. Preheat the Air Fryer to 360 o F.
2. Place the sausage and tomatoes in a baking pan and transfer in the Air Fryer.
3. Cook for about 5 minutes until done and remove the baking dish from oven.
4. Whisk together eggs with Parmesan cheese, oil, parsley, salt and black pepper and beat until combined.
5. Drizzle this mixture over sausage and tomatoes and place in the Air Fryer.
6. Cook for about 5 minutes and serve warm.

Strip Steak With Japanese Dipping Sauce

Servings: 2

Cooking Time: 40 Minutes

Ingredients:

- 2 strip steaks
- Salt and pepper to taste
- 1 tablespoon olive oil
- ½ cup soy sauce
- ½ cup rice wine vinegar
- ¼ cup grated daikon radish

Directions:

1. Preheat the Air Fryer at 3900F.
2. Place the grill pan accessory in the Air Fryer.
3. Season the steak with salt and pepper.
4. Brush with oil.
5. Grill for 20 minutes per piece and make sure to flip the beef halfway through the cooking time
6. Prepare the dipping sauce by combining the soy sauce and vinegar.
7. Serve the steak with the sauce and daikon radish.

Ham, Spinach And Egg In A Cup

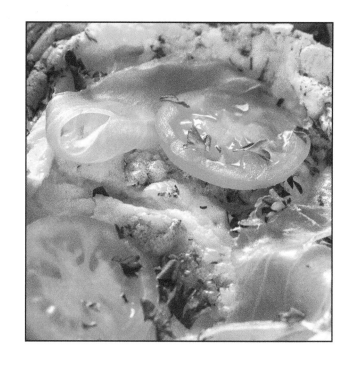

Servings: 4
Cooking Time: 20 Minutes

Ingredients:

- 1 pound fresh baby spinach
- 4 eggs
- 4 teaspoons milk
- 7-ounce ham, sliced
- 1 tablespoon unsalted butter, melted
- 1 tablespoon olive oil
- Salt and black pepper, to taste

Directions:

1. Preheat the Air Fryer to 350 o F and grease 4 ramekins with butter.
2. Heat olive oil in a skillet on medium heat and add baby spinach.
3. Cook for about 4 minutes and drain the liquid from the spinach completely.
4. Divide the spinach into the prepared ramekins and top with ham slices.
5. Crack 1 egg into each ramekin over ham slices and sprinkle evenly with milk.
6. Season with salt and black pepper and transfer into the Air Fryer.

Lunch and Dinner

Chili Bell Peppers Stew

Servings: 4
Cooking Time: 15 Minutes

Ingredients:

- 2 red bell peppers, cut into wedges
- 2 green bell peppers, cut into wedges
- 2 yellow bell peppers, cut into wedges
- ½ cup keto tomato sauce
- 1 tablespoon chili powder
- 2 teaspoons cumin, ground
- ¼ teaspoon sweet paprika
- Salt and black pepper to the taste

Directions:

1. In a pan that fits your Air Fryer, mix all the ingredients, toss, introduce the pan in the machine and cook at 370 degrees F for minutes.
2. Divide into bowls and serve for lunch.

Grilled Ham and Cheese

Servings: 2
Cooking Time: 30 Minutes

Ingredients:

- 3 low-carb buns
- 4 slices medium-cut deli ham
- 1 tbsp salted butter
- 1 oz. flour
- 3 slices cheddar cheese
- 3 slices muenster cheese

Directions:

Bread:
1. Preheat your Fryer to 350°F/175°C.
2. Mix the flour, salt and baking powder in a bowl. Put to the side.
3. Add in the butter and coconut oil to a skillet.
4. Melt for 20 seconds and pour into another bowl.
5. In this bowl, mix in the dough.
6. Scramble two eggs. Add to the dough.
7. Add ½ tablespoon of coconut flour to thicken, and place evenly into a cupcake tray. Fill about ¾ inch.
8. Bake for 20 minutes until browned.
9. Allow to cool for 15 minutes and cut each in half for the buns.

Sandwich:
1. Fry the deli meat in a skillet on a high heat.
2. Put the ham and cheese between the buns.
3. Heat the butter on medium high.
4. When brown, turn to low and add the dough to pan.
5. Press down with a weight until you smell burning, then flip to crisp both sides. Enjoy!

Thyme Green Beans

Servings: 6
Cooking Time: 20 Minutes

Ingredients:

- 1 pound green beans, trimmed and halved
- 2 eggplants, cubed
- 1 cup veggie stock
- 1 tablespoon olive oil
- 1 red chili pepper
- 1 red bell pepper, chopped
- ½ teaspoon thyme, dried
- Salt and black pepper to the taste

Directions:

1. In a pan that fits your Air Fryer, mix all the ingredients, toss, introduce the pan in the machine and cook at 350 degrees F for 20 minutes.
2. Divide into bowls and serve for lunch.

Faux Rice

Servings: 8
Cooking Time: 60 Minutes

Ingredients:

- 1 medium-to-large head of cauliflower
- ½ lemon, juiced
- garlic cloves, minced
- 2 cans mushrooms, 8 oz. each
- 1 can water chestnuts, 8 oz.
- ¾ cup peas
- ½ cup egg substitute or 1 egg, beaten
- 4 tbsp. soy sauce
- 1 tbsp. peanut oil
- 1 tbsp. sesame oil
- 1 tbsp. ginger, fresh and minced
- High quality cooking spray

Directions:

1. Mix together the peanut oil, soy sauce, sesame oil, minced ginger, lemon juice, and minced garlic to combine well.
2. Peel and wash the cauliflower head before cutting it into small florets.
3. In a food processor, pulse the florets in small batches to break them down to resemble rice grains.
4. Pour into your Air Fryer basket.
5. Drain the can of water chestnuts and roughly chop them. Pour into the basket.
6. Cook at 350°F for 20 minutes.
7. In the meantime, drain the mushrooms. When the 20 minutes are up, add the mushrooms and the peas to the fryer and continue to cook for another 15 minutes.
8. Lightly spritz a frying pan with cooking spray. Prepare an omelet with the egg substitute or the beaten egg, ensuring it is firm. Lay on a cutting board and slice it up.
9. When the cauliflower is ready, throw in the omelet and cook for an additional 5 minutes. Serve hot.

Baby Corn Pakodas

Servings: 5
Cooking Time: 20 Minutes

Ingredients:

- 1 cup flour
- ¼ tsp. baking soda
- ¼ tsp. salt
- ½ tsp. curry powder
- ½ tsp. red chili powder
- ¼ tsp. turmeric powder
- ¼ cup water
- 10 pc. baby corn, blanched

Directions:

1. Pre-heat the Air Fryer to 425°F.
2. Cover the Air Fryer basket with aluminum foil and coat with a light brushing of oil.
3. In a bowl, combine all ingredients save for the corn. Stir with a whisk until well combined.
4. Coat the corn in the batter and put inside the Air Fryer.
5. Cook for 8 minutes until a golden brown color is achieved.

Cheese and Macaroni Balls

Servings: 2
Cooking Time: 25 Minutes

Ingredients:

- 2 cups leftover macaroni
- 1 cup cheddar cheese, shredded
- 3 large eggs
- 1 cup milk
- ½ cup flour
- 1 cup bread crumbs
- ½ tsp. salt
- ¼ tsp. black pepper

Directions:

1. In a bowl, combine the leftover macaroni and shredded cheese.
2. Pour the flour in a separate bowl. Put the bread crumbs in a third bowl. Finally, in a fourth bowl, mix together the eggs and milk with a whisk.
3. With an ice-cream scoop, create balls from the macaroni mixture. Coat them the flour, then in the egg mixture, and lastly in the bread crumbs.
4. Pre-heat the Air Fryer to 365°F and cook the balls for about 10 minutes, giving them an occasional stir. Ensure they crisp up nicely.
5. Serve with the sauce of your choice.

Pulled Pork

Servings: 1
Cooking Time: 30 Minutes

Ingredients:

- 1 lb. pork tenderloin
- 2 tbsp. barbecue dry rub
- 1/3 cup heavy cream
- 1 tsp. butter

Directions:

1. Pre-heat your Fryer at 370°F.
2. Massage the dry rub of your choice into the tenderloin, coating it well.
3. Cook the tenderloin in the Fryer for twenty minutes. When cooked, shred with two forks.
4. Add the heavy cream and butter into the Fryer along with the shredded pork and stir well. Cook for a further four minutes.
5. Allow to cool a little, then serve and enjoy.

Rosemary Rib Eye Steaks

Servings: 2
Cooking Time: 40 Minutes

Ingredients:

- ¼ cup butter
- 1 clove minced garlic
- Salt and pepper
- 1 ½ tbsp. balsamic vinegar
- ¼ cup rosemary, chopped
- 2 ribeye steaks

Directions:

1. Melt the butter in a skillet over medium heat. Add the garlic and fry until fragrant.
2. Remove the skillet from the heat and add in the salt, pepper, and vinegar. Allow it to cool.
3. Add the rosemary, then pour the whole mixture into a Ziploc bag.
4. Put the ribeye steaks in the bag and shake well, making sure to coat the meat well. Refrigerate for an hour, then allow to sit for a further twenty minutes.
5. Pre-heat the Fryer at 400°F and set the rack inside. Cook the ribeyes for fifteen minutes.
6. Take care when removing the steaks from the Fryer and plate up.
7. Enjoy!

Meatballs Sandwich Delight

Servings: 4
Cooking Time: 32 Minutes

Ingredients:

- 3 baguettes; sliced more than halfway through
- 14 oz. beef; ground
- 1 tbsp. olive oil
- 1 tsp. thyme; dried
- 1 tsp. basil; dried
- 7 oz. tomato sauce
- 1 small onion; chopped
- 1 egg; whisked
- 1 tbsp. bread crumbs
- 2 tbsp. cheddar cheese; grated
- 1 tbsp. oregano; chopped
- Salt and black pepper to the taste

Directions:

1. In a bowl; combine meat with salt, pepper, onion, breadcrumbs, egg, cheese, oregano, thyme and basil; stir, shape medium meatballs and add them to your Air Fryer after you've greased it with the oil.
2. Cook them at 375 °F, for 1 minutes; flipping them halfway.
3. Add tomato sauce, cook meatballs for 10 minutes more and arrange them on sliced baguettes. Serve them right away.

Duck Fat Ribeye

Servings: 1
Cooking Time: 20 Minutes

Ingredients:

- One 16-oz ribeye steak (1 - 1 ¼ inch thick)
- 1 tbsp duck fat (or other high smoke point oil like peanut oil)
- ½ tbsp butter
- ½ tsp thyme, chopped
- Salt and pepper to taste

Directions:

1. Preheat a skillet in your Fryer at 400°F/200°C.
2. Season the steaks with the oil, salt and pepper. Remove the skillet from the Fryer once pre-heated.
3. Put the skillet on your stove top burner on a medium heat and drizzle in the oil.
4. Sear the steak for 1-minutes, depending on if you like it rare, medium or well done.
5. Turn over the steak and place in your Fryer for 6 minutes.
6. Take out the steak from your Fryer and place it back on the stove top on low heat.
7. Toss in the butter and thyme and cook for 3 minutes, basting as you go along.
8. Rest for 5 minutes and serve.

Riced Cauliflower and Curry Chicken

Servings: 6
Cooking Time: 30 Minutes

Ingredients:

- 2 lbs chicken (4 breasts)
- 1 packet curry paste
- 3 tbsp ghee (can substitute with butter)
- ½ cup heavy cream
- 1 head cauliflower (around 1 kg)

Directions:

1. In a large skillet, melt the ghee.
2. Add the curry paste and mix.
3. Once combined, add a cup of water and simmer for 5 minutes.
4. Add the chicken, cover the skillet and simmer for 18 minutes.
5. Cut a cauliflower head into florets and blend in a food processor to make the riced cauliflower.
6. When the chicken is cooked, uncover, add the cream and cook for an additional 7 minutes.
7. Serve!

Italian Sausages

Servings: 4

Cooking Time: 12 Minutes

Ingredients:

- 4 pork Italian sausages
- ½ cup keto tomato sauce
- 4 Mozzarella sticks
- 1 teaspoon butter, softened

Directions:

1. Make the cross-section in every sausage with the help of the knife.
2. Then fill the cut with the Mozzarella stick. Brush the Air Fryer pan with butter.
3. Put the stuffed sausages in the pan and sprinkle them with tomato sauce.
4. Preheat the Air Fryer to 375F.
5. Place the pan with sausages in the Air Fryer and cook them for minutes or until the sausages are golden brown.

Juicy Mexican Pork Chops

Servings: 2
Cooking Time: 25 Minutes

Ingredients:

- ¼ tsp. dried oregano
- 1 ½ tsp. taco seasoning mix
- 2 x 4-oz. boneless pork chops
- 2 tbsp. unsalted butter, divided

Directions:

1. Combine the dried oregano and taco seasoning to rub into the pork chops.
2. In your fryer, cook the chops at 400°F for fifteen minutes, turning them over halfway through to cook on the other side.
3. When the chops are a brown color, check the internal temperature has reached 145°F and remove from the Fryer. Serve with a garnish of butter.

Rosemary Salmon

Servings: 2
Cooking Time: 7 Minutes

Ingredients:

- 4 oz Feta cheese, sliced
- 1 lemon slice, chopped
- ½ teaspoon dried rosemary
- 1 teaspoon apple cider vinegar
- ½ teaspoon ground paprika
- 1-pound salmon fillet
- 1 teaspoon olive oil
- ½ teaspoon salt
- Cooking spray

Directions:

1. Rub the salmon with dried rosemary and salt.
2. Then sprinkle the fish with ground paprika and apple cider vinegar.
3. Preheat the Air Fryer to 395F.
4. Line the Air Fryer basket with baking paper and put the salmon fillet on it. Spray it with cooking spray and cook for 3 minutes.
5. Then flip the salmon on another side and cook it for 4 minutes more.
6. After this, cut the cooked salmon into 2 servings and put it on the serving plate. Top the fish with sliced feta and chopped lemon slice. Sprinkle the meal with the olive oil before serving.

Mushroom Pizza Squares

Servings: 10
Cooking Time: 20 Minutes

Ingredients:

- 1 vegan pizza dough
- 1 cup oyster mushrooms, chopped
- 1 shallot, chopped
- ¼ red bell pepper, chopped
- 2 tbsp. parsley
- Salt and pepper

Directions:

1. Pre-heat the Air Fryer at 400°F.
2. Cut the vegan pizza dough into squares.
3. In a bowl, combine the oyster mushrooms, shallot, bell pepper and parsley. Sprinkle some salt and pepper as desired.
4. Spread this mixture on top of the pizza squares.
5. Cook in the Air Fryer for 10 minutes.

Black Bean Chili

Servings: 6
Cooking Time: 25 Minutes

Ingredients:

- 1 tbsp. olive oil
- 1 medium onion, diced
- 3 cloves of garlic, minced
- 1 cup vegetable broth
- 3 cans black beans, drained and rinsed
- 2 cans diced tomatoes
- 2 chipotle peppers, chopped
- 2 tsp. cumin
- 2 tsp. chili powder
- 1 tsp. dried oregano
- ½ tsp. salt

Directions:

1. Over a medium heat, fry the garlic and onions in a little oil for 3 minutes.
2. Add in the remaining ingredients, stirring constantly and scraping the bottom to prevent sticking.
3. Pre-heat your Air Fryer at 400°F.
4. Take a heat-resistant dish small enough to fit inside the Fryer and place the mixture inside. Put a sheet of aluminum foil on top.
5. Transfer to the Air Fryer and cook for 20 minutes.
6. When ready, plate up and serve with diced avocado, chopped cilantro, and chopped tomatoes.

Salmon Skewers

Servings: 4
Cooking Time: 10 Minutes

Ingredients:

- 1-pound salmon fillet
- 4 oz bacon, sliced
- 2 mozzarella balls, sliced
- ½ teaspoon avocado oil
- ½ teaspoon chili flakes

Directions:

1. Cut the salmon into the medium size cubes (4 cubes per serving).
2. Then sprinkle salmon cubes with chili flakes and wrap in the sliced bacon.
3. String the wrapped salmon cubes on the skewers and sprinkle with avocado oil.
4. After this, preheat the Air Fryer to 400F.
5. Put the salmon skewers in the preheat Air Fryer basket and cook them at 400F for 4 minutes.
6. Then flip the skewers on another side and cook them for 6 minutes at 385F.

Cashew and Chicken Manchurian

Servings: 6
Cooking Time: 30 Minutes

Ingredients:

- 1 cup chicken boneless
- 1 spring onions, chopped
- 1 onion, chopped
- 3 green chili
- 6 cashew nuts
- 1 tsp. ginger, chopped
- ½ tsp. garlic, chopped
- 1 Egg
- 2 tbsp. flour
- 1 tbsp. cornstarch
- 1 tsp. soy sauce
- 2 tsp. chili paste
- 1 tsp. pepper
- Pinch MSG
- sugar as needed
- 1 tbsp. oil

Directions:

1. Pre-heat your Air Fryer at 360°F
2. Toss together the chicken, egg, salt and pepper to coat well.
3. Combine the cornstarch and flour and use this to cover the chicken.
4. Cook in the Fryer for 10 minutes.
5. In the meantime, toast the nuts in a frying pan. Add in the onions and cook until they turn translucent. Combine with the remaining ingredients to create the sauce.
6. Finally, add in the chicken. When piping hot, garnish with the spring onions and serve.

Almond Chicken Curry

Servings: 2
Cooking Time: 15 Minutes

Ingredients:

- 10 oz chicken fillet, chopped
- 1 teaspoon ground turmeric
- ½ cup spring onions, diced
- 1 teaspoon salt
- ½ teaspoon curry powder
- ½ teaspoon garlic, diced
- ½ teaspoon ground coriander
- ½ cup of organic almond milk
- 1 teaspoon Truvia
- 1 teaspoon olive oil

Directions:

1. Put the chicken in the bowl. Add the ground turmeric, salt, curry powder, diced garlic, ground coriander, and almond Truvia.
2. Then add olive oil and mix up the chicken.
3. After this, add almond milk and transfer the chicken in the Air Fryer pan.
4. Then preheat the Air Fryer to 375F and place the pan with korma curry inside.
5. Top the chicken with diced onion.
6. Cook the meal for minutes. Stir it after 5 minutes of cooking. If the chicken is not cooked after 10 minutes, cook it for an additional 5 minutes.

Beef Burger

Servings: 3
Cooking Time: 15 Minutes

Ingredients:

- ½ teaspoon salt
- 1 teaspoon cayenne pepper
- 1 teaspoon minced ginger
- 1 teaspoon minced garlic
- 2 tablespoons chives, chopped
- 6 lettuce leaves
- 10 oz ground beef
- 1 tablespoon avocado oil
- 1 teaspoon gochujang

Directions:

1. In the shallow bowl mix up gochujang, minced ginger, minced garlic, cayenne pepper, and salt.
2. Then mix up ground beef and churned spices mixture. Add chives and stir the ground beef mass with the help of the fork until homogenous.
3. Preheat the Air Fryer to 365F.
4. Then make 3 burgers from the ground beef mixture and put them in the Air Fryer.
5. Sprinkle the burgers with avocado oil and cook for minutes at 365F.
6. Then flip the burgers on another side and cook for 5 minutes more.

Ginger Pork

Servings: 5
Cooking Time: 20 Minutes

Ingredients:

- 16 oz pork tenderloin
- 1 tablespoon fresh ginger, chopped
- 1 red bell pepper, cut into wedges
- 1 tablespoon lemon juice
- 1 teaspoon Erythritol
- ½ cup coconut flour
- ½ teaspoon salt
- ¼ teaspoon chili powder
- ½ teaspoon minced garlic
- 3 oz celery stalk
- 2 eggs, beaten
- ¼ cup beef broth
- 1 teaspoon apple cider vinegar
- 1 tablespoon butter

Directions:

1. Chop the pork tenderloin into medium cubes and sprinkle with salt and chili powder.
2. After this, dip the pork cubes in the beaten egg and coat in the coconut flour.
3. Preheat the Air Fryer to 400F ad put the pork cubes in the Air Fryer basket. Cook them for 3 minutes.
4. When the time is finished, flip the pork cubes on another side and cook for 3 minutes more.
5. Meanwhile, make the sweet-sour sauce. Put the butter in the pan. Add apple cider vinegar, chopped celery stalk, minced garlic, lemon juice, Erythritol, bell pepper, and fresh finger. Cook the mixture over the medium heat for 6 minutes. Stir the mixture from time to time.
6. Then add beef broth and bring the mixture to boil.
7. Add the cooked pork cubes and cook the meal for 4 minutes more.

Seasoned Chicken Thighs

Servings: 4
Cooking Time: 22 Minutes

Ingredients:

- 4 chicken thighs, skinless, boneless
- 1 teaspoon jerk seasonings
- 1 teaspoon Jerk sauce
- Cooking spray

Directions:

1. Sprinkle the chicken thighs with Jerk seasonings and Jerk sauce and leave them for minutes to marinate.
2. Meanwhile, preheat the Air Fryer to 385F.
3. Place the marinated chicken thighs in the Air Fryer and spray them with the cooking spray Cook the chicken thighs for 12 minutes.
4. Then flip them on another side and cook for 10 minutes more.

Sausage and Chicken Casserole

Servings: 8
Cooking Time: 30 Minutes

Ingredients:

- 2 cloves minced garlic
- 10 eggs
- 1 cup broccoli, chopped
- ½ tbsp. salt
- 1 cup cheddar, shredded and divided
- ¼ tbsp. pepper
- ¾ cup whipping cream
- 1 x 12-oz. package cooked chicken sausage

Directions:

1. Pre-heat the Air Fryer to 400°F.
2. In a large bowl, beat the eggs with a whisk. Pour in the whipping cream and cheese. Combine well.
3. In a separate bowl, mix together the garlic, broccoli, salt, pepper and cooked sausage.
4. Place the chicken sausage mix in a casserole dish. Top with the cheese mixture.
5. Transfer to the Air Fryer and cook for about 20 minutes.

Cheesy Calzone

Servings: 2
Cooking Time: 8 Minutes

Ingredients:

- 2 tablespoons almond flour
- 2 tablespoons flax meal
- 1 tablespoon coconut oil, softened
- ¼ teaspoon salt
- ¼ teaspoon baking powder
- 2 ham slices, chopped
- 1 oz Parmesan, grated
- 1 egg yolk, whisked
- 1 tablespoon spinach, chopped
- Cooking spray

Directions:

1. Make calzone dough: mix up almond flour, flax meal, coconut oil, salt, and baking powder.
2. Knead the dough until soft and smooth.
3. Then roll it up with the help of the rolling pin and cut into halves.
4. Fill every dough half with chopped ham, grated Parmesan, and spinach.
5. Fold the dough in the shape of calzones and secure the edges.
6. Then brush calzones with the whisked egg yolk.
7. Preheat the Air Fryer basket to 350F.
8. Place the calzones in the Air Fryer basket and spray them with cooking spray. Cook them for 8 minutes or until they are light brown.
9. Flip the calzones on another side after 4 minutes of cooking.

Blue Cheese Chicken Wedges

Servings: 4
Cooking Time: 45 Minutes

Ingredients:

- Blue cheese dressing
- 2 tbsp crumbled blue cheese
- 4 strips of bacon
- 2 chicken breasts (boneless)
- 3/4 cup of your favorite buffalo sauce

Directions:

1. Boil a large pot of salted water.
2. Add in two chicken breasts to pot and cook for minutes.
3. Turn off the heat and let the chicken rest for 10 minutes. Using a fork, pull the chicken apart into strips.
4. Cook and cool the bacon strips and put to the side.
5. On a medium heat, combine the chicken and buffalo sauce. Stir until hot.
6. Add the blue cheese and buffalo pulled chicken. Top with the cooked bacon crumble.
7. Serve and enjoy.

Pork And Spinach Stew

Servings: 4
Cooking Time: 25 Minutes

Ingredients:

- 1 pound pork stew meat, cubed
- 3 garlic cloves, minced
- ¼ cup keto tomato sauce
- 1 cup spinach, torn
- ½ teaspoon olive oil

Directions:

1. In pan that fits your Air Fryer, mix the pork with the other ingredients except the spinach, toss, introduce in the Fryer and cook at 370 degrees F for minutes.
2. Add the spinach, toss, cook for 10 minutes more, divide into bowls and serve for lunch.

Parmesan Beef Mix

Servings: 4
Cooking Time: 20 Minutes

Ingredients:

- 14 ounces beef, cubed
- 7 ounces keto tomato sauce
- 1 tablespoon chives, chopped
- 2 tablespoons parmesan cheese, grated
- 1 tablespoon oregano, chopped
- 1 tablespoon olive oil
- Salt and black pepper to the taste

Directions:

1. Grease a pan that fits the Air Fryer with the oil and mix all the ingredients except the parmesan.
2. Sprinkle the parmesan on top, put the pan in the machine and cook at 380 degrees F for 20 minutes.
3. Divide between plates and serve for lunch.

Monkey Salad

Servings: 1
Cooking Time: 10 Minutes

Ingredients:

- 2 tbsp butter
- 1 cup unsweetened coconut flakes
- 1 cup raw, unsalted cashews
- 1 cup raw, unsalted s
- 1 cup 90% dark chocolate shavings

Directions:

1. In a skillet, melt the butter on a medium heat.
2. Add the coconut flakes and sauté until lightly browned for 4 minutes.
3. Add the cashews and s and sauté for minutes. Remove from the heat and sprinkle with dark chocolate shavings.
4. Serve!

I Love Bacon

Servings: 4
Cooking Time: 90 Minutes

Ingredients:

- 30 slices thick-cut bacon
- 12 oz steak
- 10 oz pork sausage
- 4 oz cheddar cheese, shredded

Directions:

1. Lay out 5 x 6 slices of bacon in a woven pattern and bake at 400°F/200°C for 20 minutes until crisp.
2. Combine the steak, bacon and sausage to form a meaty mixture.
3. Lay out the meat in a rectangle of similar size to the bacon strips. Season with salt/pepper.
4. Place the bacon weave on top of the meat mixture.
5. Place the cheese in the center of the bacon.
6. Roll the meat into a tight roll and refrigerate.
7. Make a x 7 bacon weave and roll the bacon weave over the meat, diagonally.
8. Bake at 400°F/200°C for 60 minutes or 165°F/75°C internally.
9. Let rest for 5 minutes before serving.

Amazing Beef Stew

Servings: 4
Cooking Time: 30 Minutes

Ingredients:

- 2 lbs. beef meat; cut into medium chunks
- 2 carrots; chopped
- 4 potatoes; chopped
- 1-quart veggie stock
- 1/2 tsp. smoked paprika
- A handful thyme; chopped
- Salt and black pepper to the taste

Directions:

1. In a dish that fits your Air Fryer; mix beef with carrots, potatoes, stock, salt, pepper, paprika and thyme; stir, place in Air Fryer's basket and cook at 375 °F, for 20 minutes.
2. Divide into bowls and serve right away for lunch.

French Green Beans

Servings: 4
Cooking Time: 20 Minutes

Ingredients:

- 1 ½ lb. French green beans, stems removed and blanched
- 1 tbsp. salt
- ½ lb. shallots, peeled and cut into quarters
- ½ tsp. ground white pepper
- 2 tbsp. olive oil
- ¼ cup slivered s, toasted

Directions:

1. Pre-heat the Air Fryer at 400°F.
2. Coat the vegetables with the rest of the ingredients in a bowl.
3. Transfer to the basket of your Fryer and cook for 10 minutes, making sure the green beans achieve a light brown color.

Chili Beef Bowl

Servings: 3
Cooking Time: 18 Minutes

Ingredients:

- 9 oz beef sirloin
- 1 chili pepper
- 1 green bell pepper
- ½ teaspoon minced garlic
- ¼ teaspoon ground ginger
- 1 tablespoon apple cider vinegar
- 4 tablespoons water
- ½ teaspoon salt
- 3 spring onions, chopped
- 1 teaspoon avocado oil

Directions:

1. Cut the beef sirloin into wedges.
2. Then cut bell pepper and chili pepper into wedges. Put bell pepper, chili pepper, and beef sirloin in the bowl.
3. Add minced garlic, ground ginger, apple cider vinegar, water, salt, and spring onions. Marinate the mixture for minutes.
4. Meanwhile, preheat the Air Fryer to 210F.
5. Put the bell pepper, chili pepper, and onion in the Air Fryer basket. Sprinkle them with ½ teaspoon of avocado oil and cook them for 8 minutes.
6. Transfer the cooked vegetables in 3 serving bowls.
7. After this, put the beef wedges in the Air Fryer and sprinkle them with remaining avocado oil. Cook the meat for 10 minutes at 365F. Stir it from time to time to avoid burning.
8. Meanwhile, pour the marinade from the beef and vegetables in the saucepan and bring it to boil. Simmer it for 2-3 minutes.
9. Put the cooked beef in the serving bowls.
10. Sprinkle the meal with hot marinade.

Roasted Garlic, Broccoli and Lemon

Servings: 6
Cooking Time: 25 Minutes

Ingredients:

- 2 heads broccoli, cut into florets
- 2 tsp. extra virgin olive oil
- 1 tsp. salt
- ½ tsp. black pepper
- 1 clove garlic, minced
- ½ tsp. lemon juice

Directions:

1. Cover the Air Fryer basket with aluminum foil and coat with a light brushing of oil.
2. Pre-heat the Fryer to 375°F.
3. In a bowl, combine all ingredients save for the lemon juice and transfer to the Fryer basket. Allow to cook for 15 minutes.
4. Serve with the lemon juice.

Nearly Pizza

Servings: 4
Cooking Time: 30 Minutes

Ingredients:

For Chops:

- 4 large portobello mushrooms
- 4 tsp olive oil
- 1 cup marinara sauce
- 1 cup shredded mozzarella cheese
- 10 slices sugar-free pepperoni

Directions:

1. Preheat your Fryer to 375°F/0°C.
2. De-steam the 4 mushrooms and brush each cap with the olive oil, one spoon for each cap.
3. Place on a baking sheet and bake stem side down for 8 minutes.
4. Take out of the Fryer and fill each cap with 1 cup marinara sauce, 1 cup mozzarella cheese and 3 slices of pepperoni.
5. Cook for another 10 minutes until browned.
6. Serve hot.

Beef And Green Onions Casserole

Servings: 4
Cooking Time: 21 Minutes

Ingredients:

- 10 oz lean ground beef
- 1 oz green onions, chopped
- 2 low carb tortillas
- 1 cup Mexican cheese blend, shredded
- 1 teaspoon fresh cilantro, chopped
- 1 teaspoon butter
- 1 tablespoon mascarpone
- 1 tablespoon heavy cream
- ¼ teaspoon garlic powder
- 1 teaspoon Mexican seasonings
- 1 teaspoon olive oil

Directions:

1. Pour olive oil in the skillet and heat it up over the medium heat.
2. Then add ground beef and sprinkle it with garlic powder and Mexican seasonings. Cook the ground beef for 7 minutes over the medium heat. Stir it from time to time.
3. Then chop the low carb tortillas. Grease the Air Fryer pan with butter and put the tortillas in one layer inside. Put the ground beef mixture over the tortillas and spread it gently with the help of the spoon.
4. Then sprinkle it with cilantro, green onions, mascarpone, and heavy cream. Top the casserole with Mexican cheese blend and cover with baking paper. Secure the edges of the pan well.
5. Preheat the Air Fryer to 360F.
6. Cook the casserole for minutes at 360F and then remove the baking paper and cook the meal for 5 minutes more to reach the crunchy crust.

Cauliflower Rice Chicken Curry

Servings: 4
Cooking Time: 40 Minutes

Ingredients:

- 2 lb chicken (4 breasts)
- 1 packet curry paste
- 3 tbsp ghee (can substitute with butter)
- ½ cup heavy cream
- 1 head cauliflower (around 1 kg/2.2 lb)

Directions:

1. Melt the ghee in a pot. Mix in the curry paste.
2. Add the water and simmer for 5 minutes.
3. Add the chicken, cover, and simmer on a medium heat for 20 minutes or until the chicken is cooked.
4. Shred the cauliflower florets in a food processor to resemble rice.
5. Once the chicken is cooked, uncover, and incorporate the cream.
6. Cook for 7 minutes and serve over the cauliflower.

Shrimp And Spring Onions Stew

Servings: 4
Cooking Time: 12 Minutes

Ingredients:

- 1 red bell pepper, chopped
- 14 ounces chicken stock
- 2 tablespoons keto tomato sauce
- 3 spring onions, chopped
- 1 and ½ pounds shrimp, peeled and deveined
- Salt and black pepper to the taste
- 1 tablespoon olive oil

Directions:

1. In your Air Fryer's pan greased with the oil, mix the shrimp and the other ingredients, toss, introduce the pan in the machine, and cook at 360 degrees F for minutes, stirring halfway.
2. Divide into bowls and serve for lunch.

Garlic Pork Stew

Servings: 4
Cooking Time: 30 Minutes

Ingredients:

- 1 and ½ pounds pork stew meat, cubed
- 1 red cabbage, shredded
- 1 tablespoon olive oil
- Salt and black pepper to the taste
- 2 chili peppers, chopped
- 4 garlic cloves, minced
- ½ cup veggie stock
- ¼ cup keto tomato sauce

Directions:

1. Heat up a pan that fits the Air Fryer with the oil over medium heat, add the meat, chili peppers and the garlic, stir and brown for 5 minutes.
2. Add the rest of the ingredients, toss, introduce the pan in the Fryer and cook at 380 degrees F for 20 minutes.
3. Divide the into bowls and serve for lunch.

Pork And Potatoes Recipe

Servings: 2

Cooking Time: 35 Minutes

Ingredients:

- 2 lbs. pork loin
- 2 red potatoes; cut into medium wedges
- 1/2 tsp. garlic powder
- 1/2 tsp. red pepper flakes
- 1 tsp. parsley; dried
- A drizzle of balsamic vinegar
- Salt and black pepper to the taste

Directions:

1. In your Air Fryer's pan; mix pork with potatoes, salt, pepper, garlic powder, pepper flakes, parsley and vinegar; toss and cook at 390 °F, for 25 minutes.
2. Slice pork, divide it and potatoes on plates and serve for lunch.

Mediterranean Vegetables

Servings: 4
Cooking Time: 30 Minutes

Ingredients:

- 1 cup cherry tomatoes, halved
- 1 large zucchini, sliced
- 1 green pepper, sliced
- 1 parsnip, sliced
- 1 carrot, sliced
- 1 tsp. mixed herbs
- 1 tsp. mustard
- 1 tsp. garlic puree
- 6 tbsp. olive oil
- Salt and pepper to taste

Directions:

1. Pre-heat the Air Fryer at 400°F.
2. Combine all the ingredients in a bowl, making sure to coat the vegetables well.
3. Transfer to the Fryer and cook for 6 minutes, ensuring the vegetables are tender and browned.

Potatoes And Calamari Stew

Servings: 4
Cooking Time: 16 Minutes

Ingredients:

- 10 ounces calamari, cut into strips
- 1 cup red wine
- 1 cup water
- 2 tablespoons olive oil
- 2 teaspoons pepper sauce
- 1 tablespoon hot sauce
- 1 tablespoon sweet paprika
- 1 tablespoon tomato sauce
- Salt and black pepper to taste
- ½ bunch cilantro, chopped
- 2 garlic cloves, minced
- 1 yellow onion, chopped
- 4 potatoes, cut into quarters.

Directions:

1. Place all the ingredients in a pan that fits the Air Fryer and toss.
2. Put the pan in the Fryer and cook at 400 degrees F for 16 minutes.
3. Divide the stew between bowls and serve.

Mexican Pizza

Servings: 4
Cooking Time: 15 Minutes

Ingredients:

- ¾ cup refried beans
- 1 cup salsa
- 12 frozen beef meatballs, pre-cooked
- 2 jalapeno peppers, sliced
- 6 bread
- 1 cup pepper Jack cheese, shredded
- 1 cup Colby cheese, shredded

Directions:

1. Pre-heat the Air Fryer for 4 minutes at 370°F.
2. In a bowl, mix together the salsa, meatball, jalapeno pepper and beans.
3. Place a spoonful of this mixture on top of each pita bread, along with a topping of pepper Jack and Colby cheese.
4. Bake in the Fryer for 10 minutes. Serve hot.

Cheese Pies

Servings: 4
Cooking Time: 4 Minutes

Ingredients:

- 8 wonton wraps
- 1 egg, beaten
- 1 cup cottage cheese
- 1 tablespoon Erythritol
- ½ teaspoon vanilla extract
- 1 egg white, whisked
- Cooking spray

Directions:

1. Mix up cottage cheese and Erythritol. Then add vanilla extract and egg. Stir the mixture well with the help of the fork.
2. After this, put the cottage cheese mixture on the wonton wraps and fold them in the shape of pies.
3. Then brush the pies with whisked egg white.
4. Preheat the Air Fryer to 375F.
5. Then put the cottage cheese pies in the Air Fryer and spray them with the cooking spray.
6. Cook the meal for 2 minutes from each side.

Shrimp Salad

Servings: 4
Cooking Time: 3 Minutes

Ingredients:

- 1-pound shrimps, peeled
- 1 tablespoon lemon juice
- ½ teaspoon ground cardamom
- ¼ teaspoon salt
- ½ teaspoon ground paprika
- 1 tablespoon olive oil
- 1 garlic clove, diced
- 1 avocado, peeled, pitted, chopped
- 1 teaspoon chives, chopped

Directions:

1. Put the shrimps in the big bowl. Add lemon juice, ground nutmeg, salt, and ground paprika. Mix up the shrimps and leave them for minutes to marinate.
2. Meanwhile, preheat the Air Fryer to 400F.
3. Put the marinated shrimps in the Air Fryer and cook them for 3 minutes. It is recommended to arrange shrimps in one layer.
4. Meanwhile, put the chopped avocado in the bowl and sprinkle it with diced garlic and chives.
5. Cool the shrimps to the room temperature and add in the avocado bowl.
6. Sprinkle the salad with olive oil.
7. After this, gently mix the salad with the help of two spoons.

Chicken And Cucumber Salad

Servings: 4
Cooking Time: 10 Minutes

Ingredients:

- 1 cucumber, chopped
- 1 tablespoon ricotta cheese
- 1 tablespoon mascarpone cheese
- ½ cup Monterey Jack cheese, grated
- 1-pound chicken breast, skinless, boneless
- 1 teaspoon avocado oil
- ½ teaspoon salt
- 1 teaspoon dried oregano
- 1 teaspoon ground black pepper
- 1 teaspoon ground paprika
- 1 oz bacon, chopped

Directions:

1. Rub the chicken breast with salt, dried oregano, ground black pepper, and ground paprika.
2. Then put the chopped bacon in the Air Fryer basket. Place the chicken breast over the bacon and sprinkle with avocado oil.
3. Cook the ingredients for minutes at 395F.
4. Meanwhile, in the shallow bowl mix up mascarpone cheese and ricotta cheese.
5. Put the chopped cucumber in the salad bowl. Add grated Monterey jack cheese.
6. When the chicken and bacon are cooked, remove them from the Air Fryer basket.
7. Chop the chicken breast into tiny pieces and add in the salad bowl.
8. Add bacon and mascarpone mixture.
9. Stir the salad with the help of the spatula.

Flank Steak and Avocado Butter

Servings: 1
Cooking Time: 40 Minutes

Ingredients:

- 1 flank steak
- Salt and pepper
- 2 avocados
- 2 tbsp. butter, melted
- ½ cup chimichurri sauce

Directions:

1. Rub the flank steak with salt and pepper to taste and leave to sit for twenty minutes.
2. Pre-heat the Fryer at 400°F and place a rack inside.
3. Halve the avocados and take out the pits. Spoon the flesh into a bowl and mash with a fork. Mix in the melted butter and chimichurri sauce, making sure everything is well combined.
4. Put the steak in the Fryer and cook for six minutes. Flip over and allow to cook for another six minutes.
5. Serve the steak with the avocado butter and enjoy!

Fried Potatoes

Servings: 1
Cooking Time: 55 Minutes

Ingredients:

- 1 medium russet potatoes, scrubbed and peeled
- 1 tsp. olive oil
- ¼ tsp. onion powder
- 1/8 tsp. salt
- A dollop of vegan butter
- A dollop of vegan cream cheese
- 1 tbsp. Kalamata olives
- 1 tbsp. chives, chopped

Directions:

1. Pre-heat the Air Fryer at 400°F.
2. In a bowl, coat the potatoes with the onion powder, salt, olive oil, and vegan butter.
3. Transfer to the Fryer and allow to cook for 40 minutes, turning the potatoes over at the halfway point.
4. Take care when removing the potatoes from the Fryer and enjoy with the vegan cream cheese, Kalamata olives and chives on top, plus any other vegan sides you desire.

Beef And Tomato Mix

Servings: 4
Cooking Time: 25 Minutes

Ingredients:

- 1 and ½ pounds beef stew meat, cubed
- ½ cup green onions, chopped
- 3 tablespoons butter, melted
- ½ cup celery stalks, chopped
- 1 garlic clove, minced
- ½ teaspoon Italian seasoning
- 15 ounces keto tomato sauce
- Salt and black pepper to the taste

Directions:

1. Heat up a pan that fits your Air Fryer with the butter over medium heat, add the meat, toss and brown for 5 minutes.
2. Add the rest of the ingredients, toss, introduce the pan in the Fryer and cook at 390 degrees F for 20 minutes.
3. Divide into bowls and serve for lunch.

'No Potato' Shepherd's Pie

Servings: 6
Cooking Time: 70 Minutes

Ingredients:

- 1 lb lean ground beef
- 8 oz low-carb mushroom sauce mix
- ¼ cup ketchup
- 1 lb package frozen mixed vegetables
- 1 lb Aitkin's low-carb bake mix or equivalent

Directions:

1. Preheat your Fryer to 375°F/0°C.
2. Prepare the bake mix according to package.
3. Layer into the skillet base.
4. Cut the dough into triangles and roll them from base to tip. Set to the side.
5. Brown the ground beef with the salt. Stir in the mushroom sauce, ketchup and mixed vegetables.
6. Bring the mixture to the boil and reduce the heat to medium, cover and simmer until tender.
7. Put the dough triangles on top of the mixture, tips pointing towards the center.
8. Bake for 60 minutes until piping hot and serve!

Mustard Chicken

Servings: 4
Cooking Time: 30 Minutes

Ingredients:

- 1 and ½ pounds chicken thighs, bone-in
- 2 tablespoons Dijon mustard
- A pinch of salt and black pepper
- Cooking spray

Directions:

1. In a bowl, mix the chicken thighs with all the other ingredients and toss.
2. Put the chicken in your Air Fryer's basket and cook at 370 degrees F for 30 minutes shaking halfway.
3. Serve these chicken thighs for lunch.

Snack and Appetizers

Italian-Style Tomato Parmesan Crisps

Servings: 4
Cooking Time: 20 Minutes

Ingredients:

- 4 Roma tomatoes, sliced
- 2 tablespoons olive oil
- Sea salt and white pepper, to taste
- 1 teaspoon Italian seasoning mix
- 4 tablespoons Parmesan cheese, grated

Directions:

1. Start by preheating your Air Fryer to 350 degrees F. Generously grease the Air Fryer basket with nonstick cooking oil.
2. Toss the sliced tomatoes with the remaining ingredients. Transfer them to the cooking basket without overlapping.
3. Cook in the preheated Air Fryer for 5 minutes. Shake the cooking basket and cook an additional 5 minutes. Work in batches.
4. Serve with Mediterranean aioli for dipping, if desired. Bon appétit!

Cheddar Cheese Breadsticks

Servings: 6
Cooking Time: 30 Minutes

Ingredients:

- 1/2 cup almond meal
- Sea salt and ground black pepper, to taste
- 1/4 teaspoon smoked paprika
- 1/2 teaspoon celery seeds
- 6 ounces mature Cheddar, cold, freshly grated
- 2 tablespoons cream cheese
- 2 tablespoons cold butter

Directions:

1. Start by preheating your Air Fryer to 330 degrees F. Line the Air Fryer basket with parchment paper.
2. In a mixing bowl, thoroughly combine the almond meal, salt, black pepper, paprika, and celery seeds.
3. Then, combine the cheese and butter in the bowl of a stand mixer. Slowly stir in the almond meal mixture and mix to combine well.
4. Then, pack the batter into a cookie press fitted with a star disk. Pipe the long ribbons of dough across the parchment paper. Then cut into six-inch lengths.
5. Bake in the preheated Air Fryer for 1 minutes.
6. Repeat with the remaining dough. Let the cheese straws cool on a rack. You can store them between sheets of parchment in an airtight container. Bon appétit!

Smoked Almonds

Servings: 6
Cooking Time: 6 Minutes

Ingredients:

- 1 cup almonds
- 1/4 tsp cumin
- 1 tsp chili powder
- 1/4 tsp smoked paprika
- 2 tsp olive oil

Directions:

1. Add almond into the bowl and remaining ingredients and toss to coat.
2. Transfer almonds into the Air Fryer basket and cook at 3 F for 6 minutes. Shake halfway through.
3. Serve and enjoy.

Instant Potato Croquettes

Servings: 4
Cooking Time: 8 Minutes

Ingredients:

- 2 medium Russet potatoes, boiled, peeled and mashed
- 2 tablespoons all-purpose flour
- ½ cup Parmesan cheese, grated
- 3 eggs
- ½ cup breadcrumbs
- 2 tablespoons vegetable oil
- Pinch of ground nutmeg
- Salt and black pepper, to taste

Directions:

1. Mix together potatoes with egg yolk, Parmesan, nutmeg, salt and black pepper.
2. Make equal sized small balls from this mixture and keep aside.
3. Whisk the eggs in a shallow dish.
4. Mix together oil and breadcrumbs in another shallow dish.
5. Dip the croquettes evenly in the eggs and dredge in the breadcrumb mixture.
6. Place the croquettes in an Air Fryer basket and cook for about 8 minutes and dish out to serve warm.

Feta And Parsley Filo Triangles

Servings: 6
Cooking Time: 5 Minutes

Ingredients:

- 1 egg yolk
- 4-ounce feta cheese, crumbled
- 1 scallion, chopped finely
- 2 tablespoons fresh parsley, chopped finely
- 2 frozen filo pastry sheets, thawed and cut into three strips
- 2 tablespoons olive oil
- Salt and black pepper, to taste

Directions:

1. Preheat the Air Fryer to 390 o F and grease an Air Fryer basket.
2. Whisk egg yolk in a large bowl and beat well.
3. Stir in feta cheese, scallion, parsley, salt and black pepper.
4. Brush pastry with olive oil and put a tablespoon of feta mixture over one corner of filo strip.
5. Fold diagonally to create a triangle and keep folding until filling is completely wrapped.
6. Repeat with the remaining strips and filling and coat the triangles with olive oil.
7. Place the triangles in the Air Fryer basket and cook for about 3 minutes.
8. Now, set the Air Fryer to 360 degrees F and cook for another 2 minutes.
9. Dish out and serve warm.

Celery Chips With Harissa Mayonnaise Sauce

Servings: 3
Cooking Time: 30 Minutes

Ingredients:

- 1/2 pound celery root
- 2 tablespoons olive oil
- Sea salt and ground black pepper, to taste
- Harissa Mayo
- 1/4 cup mayonnaise
- 2 tablespoons sour cream
- 1/2 tablespoon harissa paste
- 1/4 teaspoon ground cumin
- Salt, to taste

Directions:

1. Cut the celery root into desired size and shape.
2. Then, preheat your Air Fryer to 400 degrees F. Now, spritz the Air Fryer basket with cooking spray.
3. Toss the celery chips with the olive oil, salt, and black pepper. Bake in the preheated Air Fryer for 25 to minutes, turning them over every 10 minutes to promote even cooking.
4. Meanwhile, mix all ingredients for the harissa mayo. Place in your refrigerator until ready to serve. Bon appétit!

Broccoli Pop-Corn

Servings: 4
Cooking Time: 6 Minutes

Ingredients:

- 2 cups broccoli florets
- 2 cups coconut flour
- 1/4 cup butter, melted
- 4 eggs yolks
- Pepper Salt

Directions:

1. In a bowl whisk egg yolk with melted butter, pepper, and salt. Add coconut flour and stir to combine.
2. Preheat the Air Fryer to 400 F.
3. Spray Air Fryer basket with cooking spray.
4. Coat each broccoli floret with egg mixture and place into the Air Fryer basket and cook for 6 minutes.
5. Serve and enjoy.

Mediterranean Style Cocktail Meatballs

Servings: 4
Cooking Time: 15 Minutes

Ingredients:

For the Meatballs:

- 1 1/2 tablespoons melted butter
- 2 teaspoons red pepper flakes, crushed
- ½ tablespoon fresh cilantro, finely chopped
- 2 eggs
- 2 tablespoons fresh mint leaves, finely chopped
- 1 teaspoon kosher salt
- 4 garlic cloves, finely minced
- 1 pound ground pork
- 2 tablespoons capers

For Mediterranean Dipping sauce:

- 1/3 cup black olives, pitted and finely chopped
- 2 tablespoons fresh Italian parsley
- 1/2 teaspoon lemon zest
- 1/3 cup Greek-style yogurt
- 1/2 teaspoon dill, fresh or dried and chopped
- 2 tablespoons fresh rosemary

Directions:

1. Start by preheating your Air Fryer to 395 degrees F.
2. In a large-sized mixing dish, place all ingredients for the meatballs; mix to combine well. Shape the mixture into golf ball sized meatballs.
3. Cook the meatballs for about 9 minutes, working in batches.
4. In the meantime, make the dipping sauce by thoroughly whisking all the sauce ingredients.
5. Serve warm meatballs with the prepared Mediterranean dipping sauce.

Old-Fashioned Onion Rings

Servings: 4
Cooking Time: 10 Minutes

Ingredients:

- 1 large onion, cut into rings
- 1 ¼ cups all-purpose flour
- 1 cup milk
- 1 egg
- ¾ cup dry bread crumbs
- Salt, to taste

Directions:

1. Preheat the Air Fryer to 360 o F and grease the Air Fryer basket.
2. Mix together flour and salt in a dish.
3. Whisk egg with milk in a second dish until well mixed.
4. Place the breadcrumbs in a third dish.
5. Coat the onion rings with the flour mixture and dip into the egg mixture.
6. Lastly dredge in the breadcrumbs and transfer the onion rings in the Air Fryer basket.
7. Cook for about 10 minutes and dish out to serve warm.

Crunchy Bacon Bites

Servings: 4
Cooking Time: 10 Minutes

Ingredients:

- 4 bacon strips, cut into small pieces
- 1/2 cup pork rinds, crushed
- 1/4 cup hot sauce

Directions:

1. Add bacon pieces in a bowl.
2. Add hot sauce and toss well.
3. Add crushed pork rinds and toss until bacon pieces are well coated.
4. Transfer bacon pieces in Air Fryer basket and cook at 350 F for 10 minutes.
5. Serve and enjoy.

Avocado Fries

Servings: 4
Cooking Time: 20 Minutes

Ingredients:

- ½ cup panko
- ½ tsp. salt
- 1 whole avocado
- 1 oz. aquafaba

Directions:

1. In a shallow bowl, stir together the panko and salt.
2. In a separate shallow bowl, add the aquafaba.
3. Dip the avocado slices into the aquafaba, before coating each one in the panko.
4. Place the slices in your Air Fryer basket, taking care not to overlap any. Air fry for 10 minutes at 390°F.

Cheesy Zucchini Sticks

Servings: 2
Cooking Time: 20 Minutes

Ingredients:

- 1 zucchini, slice into strips
- 2 tablespoons mayonnaise
- 1/4 cup tortilla chips, crushed
- 1/4 cup Romano cheese, shredded
- Sea salt and black pepper, to your liking
- 1 tablespoon garlic powder
- 1/2 teaspoon red pepper flakes

Directions:

1. Coat the zucchini with mayonnaise.
2. Mix the crushed tortilla chips, cheese and spices in a shallow dish.
3. Then, coat the zucchini sticks with the cheese/chips mixture.
4. Cook in the preheated Air Fryer at 0 degrees F for 12 minutes, shaking the basket halfway through the cooking time.
5. Work in batches until the sticks are crispy and golden brown. Bon appétit!

Zucchini Chips

Servings: 2
Cooking Time: 30 Minutes

Ingredients:

- 3 medium zucchini, sliced
- 1 tsp. parsley, chopped
- 3 tbsp. parmesan cheese, grated
- Pepper to taste
- Salt to taste

Directions:

1. Pre-heat the Air Fryer to 425°F.
2. Put the sliced zucchini on a sheet of baking paper and spritz with cooking spray.
3. Combine the cheese, pepper, parsley, and salt. Use this mixture to sprinkle over the zucchini.
4. Transfer to the Air Fryer and cook for 25 minutes, ensuring the zucchini slices have crisped up nicely before serving.

Basic Salmon Croquettes

Servings: 16
Cooking Time: 14 Minutes

Ingredients:

- 1 large can red salmon, drained
- 2 eggs, lightly beaten
- 2 tablespoons fresh parsley, chopped
- 1 cup breadcrumbs
- 2 tablespoons milk
- Salt and black pepper, to taste
- 1/3 cup vegetable oil

Directions:

1. Preheat the Air Fryer to 390 o F and grease an Air Fryer basket.
2. Mash the salmon completely in a bowl and stir in eggs, parsley, breadcrumbs, milk, salt and black pepper.
3. Mix until well combined and make 16 equal-sized croquettes from the mixture.
4. Mix together oil and breadcrumbs in a shallow dish and coat the croquettes in this mixture.
5. Place half of the croquettes in the Air Fryer basket and cook for about 7 minutes.
6. Repeat with the remaining croquettes and serve warm.

Pumpkin Seeds

Servings: 1 ½ Cups
Cooking Time: 55 Minutes

Ingredients:

- 1 ½ cups pumpkin seeds from a large whole pumpkin
- Olive oil
- 1 ½ tsp. salt
- 1 tsp. smoked paprika

Directions:

1. Boil two quarts of well-salted water in a pot. Cook the pumpkin seeds in the boiling water for 10 minutes.
2. Dump the content of the pot into a sieve and dry the seeds on paper towels for at least 20 minutes.
3. Pre-heat the Air Fryer to 350°F.
4. Cover the seeds with olive oil, salt and smoked paprika, before placing them in the Air Fryer basket.
5. Air fry for 35 minutes. Give the basket a good shake several times throughout the cooking process to ensure the pumpkin seeds are crispy and lightly browned.
6. Let the seeds cool before serving. Alternatively, you can keep them in an air-tight container or bag for snacking or for use as a yogurt topping.

Green Beans and S

Servings: 4
Cooking Time: 15 Minutes

Ingredients:

- 1 lb fresh green beans, trimmed
- 2 tbsp butter
- ¼ cup sliced s
- 2 tsp lemon pepper

Directions:

1. Steam the green beans for 8 minutes, until tender, then drain.
2. On a medium heat, melt the butter in a skillet.
3. Sauté the s until browned.
4. Sprinkle with salt and pepper.
5. Mix in the green beans.

Mexican-Style Corn On The Cob With Bacon

Servings: 4
Cooking Time: 20 Minutes

Ingredients:

- 2 slices bacon
- 4 ears fresh corn, shucked and cut into halves
- 1 avocado, pitted, peeled and mashed
- 1 teaspoon ancho chili powder
- 2 garlic cloves
- 2 tablespoons cilantro, chopped
- 1 teaspoon lime juice
- Salt and black pepper, to taste

Directions:

1. Start by preheating your Air Fryer to 400 degrees F. Cook the bacon for 6 to 7 minutes; chop into small chunks and reserve.
2. Spritz the corn with cooking spray. Cook at 395 degrees F for 8 minutes, turning them over halfway through the cooking time.
3. Mix the reserved bacon with the remaining ingredients. Spoon the bacon mixture over the corn on the cob and serve immediately. Bon appétit!

Old-Fashioned Eggplant Slices

Servings: 2
Cooking Time: 26 Minutes

Ingredients:

- 1 medium eggplant, peeled and cut into
- ½-inch round slices
- ½ cup all-purpose flour
- 1 cup Italian-style breadcrumbs
- 2 eggs, beaten
- 2 tablespoons milk
- Salt, to taste
- ¼ cup olive oil

Directions:

1. Preheat the Air Fryer to 390 o F and grease in an Air Fryer basket.
2. Season the eggplant slices with salt and keep aside for 1 hour.
3. Place flour in a shallow dish.
4. Whisk the eggs with milk in a second dish.
5. Mix together oil and breadcrumbs in a third shallow dish.
6. Coat the eggplant slices evenly with flour, then dip in the egg mixture and finally coat with breadcrumb mixture.
7. Transfer the eggplant slices in the Air Fryer basket and cook for about 8 minutes.
8. Dish out and serve warm.

Fried Pickle Chips With Greek Yogurt Dip

Servings: 5
Cooking Time: 20 Minutes

Ingredients:

- 1/2 cup cornmeal
- 1/2 cup all-purpose flour
- 1 teaspoon cayenne pepper
- 1/2 teaspoon shallot powder
- 1 teaspoon garlic powder
- 1/2 teaspoon porcini powder
- Kosher salt and ground black pepper, to taste
- 2 eggs
- 2 cups pickle chips, pat dry with kitchen towels

Greek Yogurt Dip:

- 1/2 cup Greek yogurt
- 1 clove garlic, minced
- 1/4 teaspoon ground black pepper
- 1 tablespoon fresh chives, chopped

Directions:

1. In a shallow bowl, mix the cornmeal and flour; add the seasonings and mix to combine well. Beat the eggs in a separate shallow bowl.
2. Dredge the pickle chips in the flour mixture, then, in the egg mixture. Press the pickle chips into the flour mixture again, coating evenly.
3. Cook in the preheated Air Fryer at 400 degrees F for 5 minutes; shake the basket and cook for 5 minutes more. Work in batches.
4. Meanwhile, mix all the sauce ingredients until well combined.
5. Serve the fried pickles with the Greek yogurt dip and enjoy.

Cilantro Shrimp Balls

Servings: 4
Cooking Time: 15 Minutes

Ingredients:

- 1 pound shrimp, peeled, deveined and minced
- 1 egg, whisked
- 3 tablespoons coconut, shredded
- ½ cup coconut flour
- 1 tablespoon avocado oil
- 1 tablespoon cilantro, chopped

Directions:

1. In a bowl, mix all the ingredients, stir well and shape medium balls out of this mix.
2. Place the balls in your lined Air Fryer's basket, cook at 350 degrees F for minutes and serve as an appetizer.

Bacon Filled Poppers

Servings: 4
Cooking Time: 15 Minutes

Ingredients:

- 4 strips crispy cooked bacon
- 3 tablespoons butter
- ½ cup jalapeno peppers, diced
- 2/3 cup almond flour
- 2 oz. Cheddar cheese, white, shredded
- 1 pinch cayenne pepper
- 1 tablespoon bacon fat
- 1 teaspoon kosher salt
- Black pepper, ground, to taste

Directions:

1. Preheat the Air Fryer to 390 o F and grease an Air Fryer basket.
2. Mix together butter with salt and water on medium heat in a skillet.
3. Whisk in the flour and sauté for about minutes.
4. Dish out in a bowl and mix with the remaining ingredients to form a dough.
5. Wrap plastic wrap around the dough and refrigerate for about half an hour.
6. Make small popper balls out of this dough and arrange in the Air Fryer basket.
7. Cook for about 15 minutes and dish out to serve warm.

Veggie Pastries

Servings: 8
Cooking Time: 37 Minutes

Ingredients:

- 2 large potatoes, peeled
- 1 tablespoon olive oil
- ½ cup carrot, peeled and chopped
- ½ cup onion, chopped
- 2 garlic cloves, minced
- 2 tablespoons fresh ginger, minced
- ½ cup green peas, shelled
- Salt and ground black pepper, as needed
- 3 puff pastry sheets

Directions:

1. In the pan of a boiling water, put the potatoes and cook for about 20 minutes.
2. Drain the potatoes well and with a potato masher, mash the potatoes.
3. In a skillet, heat the oil over medium heat and sauté the carrot, onion, ginger, and garlic for about 4-5 minutes.
4. Drain all the fat from the skillet.
5. Stir in the mashed potatoes, peas, salt, and black pepper. Cook for about 1-2 minutes.
6. Once done, remove the potato mixture from heat and set aside to cool completely.
7. Put the puff pastry onto a smooth surface.
8. Cut each puff pastry sheet into four pieces and then cut each piece in a round shape.
9. Add about two tablespoons of veggie filling over each pastry round.
10. Moisten the edges using your wet fingers.
11. Fold each pastry round in half to seal the filling.
12. Using a fork, firmly press the edges.
13. Set the temperature of Air Fryer to 390 degrees F.
14. Add the pastries in an Air Fryer basket in a single layer in 2 batches.
15. Air Fry for about 5 minutes.
16. Serve.

Decadent Brie And Pork Meatballs

Servings: 8
Cooking Time: 25 Minutes

Ingredients:

- 1 teaspoon cayenne pepper
- 2 teaspoons mustard
- 2 tablespoons Brie cheese, grated
- 5 garlic cloves, minced
- 2 small-sized yellow onions, peeled and chopped
- 1 ½ pounds ground pork
- Sea salt and freshly ground black pepper, to taste

Directions:

1. Mix all of the above ingredients until everything is well incorporated.
2. Now, form the mixture into balls (the size of golf a ball).
3. Cook for 17 minutes at 5 degrees F.
4. Serve with your favorite sauce.

Crab Mushrooms

Servings: 16
Cooking Time: 8 Minutes

Ingredients:

- 16 mushrooms, clean and chop stems
- 1/4 tsp chili powder
- 1/4 tsp onion powder
- 1/4 cup mozzarella cheese, shredded
- 2 oz crab meat, chopped
- 8 oz cream cheese, softened
- 2 tsp garlic, minced
- 1/4 tsp pepper

Directions:

1. In a mixing bowl, mix together stems, chili powder, onion powder, pepper, cheese, crabmeat, cream cheese, and garlic until well combined.
2. Stuff mushrooms with bowl mixture and place into the Air Fryer basket.
3. Cook mushrooms at 0 F for 8 minutes.
4. Serve and enjoy.

Perfect Crab Dip

Servings: 4
Cooking Time: 7 Minutes

Ingredients:

- 1 cup crabmeat
- 2 tbsp parsley, chopped
- 2 tbsp fresh lemon juice
- 2 tbsp hot sauce
- 1/2 cup green onion, sliced
- 2 cups cheese, grated
- 1/4 cup mayonnaise
- 1/4 tsp pepper
- 1/2 tsp salt

Directions:

1. In a 6-inch dish, mix together crabmeat, hot sauce, cheese, mayo, pepper, and salt.
2. Place dish in Air Fryer basket and cook dip at 400 F for 7 minutes.
3. Remove dish from air fryer.
4. Drizzle dip with lemon juice and garnish with parsley.
5. Serve and enjoy.

Crunchy Roasted Pepitas

Servings: 4
Cooking Time: 20 Minutes

Ingredients:

- 2 cups fresh pumpkin seeds with shells
- 1 tablespoon olive oil
- 1 teaspoon sea salt
- 1 teaspoon ground coriander
- 1 teaspoon cayenne pepper

Directions:

1. Toss the pumpkin seeds with the olive oil.
2. Spread in an even layer in the Air Fryer basket; roast the seeds at 350 degrees F for 15 minutes, shaking the basket every 5 minutes.
3. Immediately toss the seeds with the salt, coriander, salt, and cayenne pepper. Enjoy!

Flavorful Pork Meatballs

Servings: 4
Cooking Time: 10 Minutes

Ingredients:

- 2 eggs, lightly beaten
- 2 tbsp capers
- 1/2 lb ground pork
- 3 garlic cloves, minced
- 2 tbsp fresh mint, chopped
- 1/2 tbsp cilantro, chopped
- 2 tsp red pepper flakes, crushed
- 1 1/2 tbsp butter, melted
- 1 tsp kosher salt

Directions:

1. Preheat the Air Fryer to 395 F.
2. Add all ingredients into the mixing bowl and mix until well combined.
3. Spray Air Fryer basket with cooking spray.
4. Make small balls from meat mixture and place into the Air Fryer basket.
5. Cook meatballs for 10 minutes. Shake basket halfway through.
6. Serve and enjoy.

Hot Cheesy Dip

Servings: 6
Cooking Time: 12 Minutes

Ingredients:

- 12 ounces coconut cream
- 2 teaspoons keto hot sauce
- 8 ounces cheddar cheese, grated

Directions:

1. In ramekin, mix the cream with hot sauce and cheese and whisk.
2. Put the ramekin in the Fryer and cook at 390 degrees F for minutes.
3. Whisk, divide into bowls and serve as a dip.

Maple Glazed Beets

Servings: 8
Cooking Time: 60 Minutes

Ingredients:

- 3 ½ lb. beetroots
- 4 tbsp. maple syrup
- 1 tbsp. coconut oil

Directions:

1. Wash and peel the beets. Cut them up into 1-inch pieces.
2. Put the coconut oil in the Air Fryer and melt for 1 minute at 320°F.
3. Place the beet cubes to the Air Fryer Basket and allow to cook for 40 minutes. Coat the beetroots in two tbsp. of the maple syrup and cook for another 10 minutes, ensuring the beets become soft.
4. Toss the cooked beets with the remaining two tbsp. of maple syrup and serve right away.

Sweet Potato Wedges

Servings: 2
Cooking Time: 25 Minutes

Ingredients:

- 2 large sweet potatoes, cut into wedges
- 1 tbsp. olive oil
- 1 tsp. chili powder
- 1 tsp. mustard powder
- 1 tsp. cumin
- 1 tbsp. Mexican seasoning Pepper to taste
- Salt to taste

Directions:

1. Pre-heat the Air Fryer at 350°F.
2. Place all of the ingredients into a bowl and combine well to coat the sweet potatoes entirely.
3. Place the wedges in the Air Fryer basket and air fry for 20 minutes, shaking the basket at 5 minute intervals.

Crab Dip

Servings: 4
Cooking Time: 20 Minutes

Ingredients:

- 8 ounces cream cheese, soft
- 1 tablespoon lemon juice
- 1 cup coconut cream
- 1 tablespoon lemon juice
- 1 bunch green onions, minced
- 1 pound artichoke hearts, drained and chopped
- 12 ounces jumbo crab meat
- A pinch of salt and black pepper
- 1 and ½ cups mozzarella, shredded

Directions:

1. In a bowl, combine all the ingredients except half of the cheese and whisk them really well.
2. Transfer this to a pan that fits your Air Fryer, introduce in the machine and cook at 400 degrees F for minutes.
3. Sprinkle the rest of the mozzarella on top and cook for 5 minutes more.
4. Divide the mix into bowls and serve as a party dip.

Simple Radish Chips

Servings: 12
Cooking Time: 15 Minutes

Ingredients:

- 1 lb radish, wash and slice into chips
- 2 tbsp olive oil
- 1/4 tsp pepper
- 1 tsp salt

Directions:

1. Preheat the Air Fryer to 375 F.
2. Add all ingredients into the large bowl and toss well.
3. Add radish slices into the Air Fryer basket and cook for 15 minutes. Shake basket 2-times while cooking.
4. Serve and enjoy.

Cauliflower Poppers

Servings: 6
Cooking Time: 16 Minutes

Ingredients:

- 1 large head cauliflower, cut into bite-sized florets
- 2 tablespoons olive oil
- Salt and freshly ground black pepper, as needed

Directions:

1. Drizzle the cauliflower florets with oil.
2. Sprinkle with salt and black pepper.
3. Set the temperature of Air Fryer to 0 degrees F.
4. Place the cauliflower florets in a greased Air Fryer basket in a single layer in 2 batches.
5. Air Fry for about 8 minutes, shaking once halfway through.
6. Serve hot.

Basil Pork Bites

Servings: 6
Cooking Time: 25 Minutes

Ingredients:

- 2 pounds pork belly, cut into strips
- 2 tablespoons olive oil
- 2 teaspoons fennel seeds
- A pinch of salt and black pepper
- A pinch of basil, dried

Directions:

1. In a bowl, mix all the ingredients, toss and put the pork strips in your Air Fryer's basket and cook at 425 degrees F for 25 minutes.
2. Divide into bowls and serve as a snack.

Grilled Tomatoes

Servings: 2
Cooking Time: 25 Minutes

Ingredients:

- 2 tomatoes, medium to large
- Herbs of your choice, to taste
- Pepper to taste
- High quality cooking spray

Directions:

1. Wash and dry the tomatoes, before chopping them in half.
2. Lightly spritz them all over with cooking spray.
3. Season each half with herbs (oregano, basil, parsley, rosemary, thyme, sage, etc.) as desired and black pepper.
4. Put the halves in the tray of your Air Fryer. Cook for 20 minutes at 320°F, or longer if necessary. Larger tomatoes will take longer to cook.

Easy Habanero Wings

Servings: 6
Cooking Time: 25 Minutes

Ingredients:

- 3 cloves garlic, peeled and halved
- 2 tablespoons habanero hot sauce
- 1/2 tablespoon soy sauce
- 1 ½ pounds chicken wings
- 1 teaspoon garlic salt
- 1 teaspoon smoked cayenne pepper
- 1 teaspoon freshly ground black pepper, or to taste

Directions:

1. Rub the chicken wings with the garlic.
2. Then, season them with the salt, black pepper, and the smoked cayenne pepper.
3. Transfer the chicken wings to the food basket; add the soy sauce, habanero hot sauce, and honey; toss to coat on all sides.
4. Air-fry the chicken wings at 5 degrees F for 16 minutes or until warmed through.

Lemon Tofu

Servings: 4
Cooking Time: 15 Minutes

Ingredients:

- 1 lb tofu, drained and pressed
- 1 tbsp arrowroot powder
- 1 tbsp tamari

For sauce:

- 2 tsp arrowroot powder
- 2 tbsp erythritol
- 1/2 cup water
- 1/3 cup lemon juice
- 1 tsp lemon zest

Directions:

1. Cut tofu into cubes. Add tofu and tamari into the zip-lock bag and shake well.
2. Add 1 tbsp arrowroot into the bag and shake well to coat the tofu. Set aside for 15 minutes.
3. Meanwhile, in a bowl, mix together all sauce ingredients and set aside.
4. Spray Air Fryer basket with cooking spray.
5. Add tofu into the Air Fryer basket and cook at 390 F for 10 minutes. Shake halfway through.
6. Add cooked tofu and sauce mixture into the pan and cook over medium-high heat for 3-5 minutes.
7. Serve and enjoy.

Butternut Squash Fries

Servings: 2
Cooking Time: 40 Minutes

Ingredients:

- 2 pounds butternut squash, peeled and cut into ½ inch strips
- 1 teaspoon chili powder
- ½ teaspoon ground cinnamon
- ¼ teaspoon garlic salt

Directions:

1. Preheat the Air Fryer to 390 o F and grease an Air Fryer basket
2. Season butternut squash with all other ingredients in a bowl until well combined.
3. Arrange half of the squash fries in the Air Fryer basket and cook for about 20 minutes.
4. Repeat with the remaining fries and dish out to serve warm.

Crispy Eggplant Slices

Servings: 4
Cooking Time: 16 Minutes

Ingredients:

- 1 medium eggplant, peeled and cut into ½-inch round slices
- Salt, as required
- ½ cup all-purpose flour
- 2 eggs, beaten
- 1 cup Italian-style breadcrumbs
- ¼ cup olive oil

Directions:

1. In a colander, add the eggplant slices and sprinkle with salt.
2. Set aside for about 45 minutes and pat dry the eggplant slices.
3. Add the flour in a shallow dish.
4. Crack the eggs in a second dish and beat well.
5. In a third dish, mix together the oil, and breadcrumbs.
6. Coat each eggplant slice with flour, then dip into beaten eggs and finally, evenly coat with the breadcrumbs mixture.
7. Set the temperature of Air Fryer to 390 degrees F.
8. Arrange the eggplant slices in an Air Fryer basket in a single layer in 2 batches.
9. Air Fry for about 8 minutes.
10. Serve.

Nutty Cauliflower Poppers

Servings: 4
Cooking Time: 12 Minutes

Ingredients:

- ¼ cup golden raisins
- 1 cup boiling water
- ¼ cup toasted pine nuts
- 1 head of cauliflower, cut into small florets
- ½ cup olive oil, divided
- 1 tablespoon curry powder
- ¼ teaspoon salt

Directions:

1. Preheat the Air Fryer to 390 o F and grease an Air Fryer basket.
2. Put raisins in boiling water in a bowl and keep aside.
3. Drizzle 1 teaspoon olive oil on the pine nuts in another bowl.
4. Place the pine nuts in an Air Fryer basket and cook for about 2 minutes.
5. Remove the pine nuts from the Air Fryer and keep aside.
6. Mix together cauliflower, salt, curry powder and remaining olive oil in a large bowl.
7. Transfer this mixture into the Air Fryer basket and cook for about 12 minutes
8. Dish out the cauliflower in a serving bowl and stir in the pine nuts.
9. Drain raisins and add to the serving bowl.

Broccoli Florets

Servings: 4
Cooking Time: 20 Minutes

Ingredients:

- 1 lb. broccoli, cut into florets
- 1 tbsp. lemon juice
- 1 tbsp. olive oil
- 1 tbsp. sesame seeds
- 3 garlic cloves, minced

Directions:

1. In a bowl, combine all of the ingredients, coating the broccoli well.
2. Transfer to the Air Fryer basket and air fry at 400°F for 13 minutes.

Brussels Sprouts

Servings: 2
Cooking Time: 15 Minutes

Ingredients:

- 2 cups Brussels sprouts, sliced in half
- 1 tbsp. balsamic vinegar
- 1 tbsp. olive oil
- ¼ tsp. salt

Directions:

1. Toss all of the ingredients together in a bowl, coating the Brussels sprouts well.
2. Place the sprouts in the Air Fryer basket and air fry at 400°F for 10 minutes, shaking the basket at the halfway point.

Turmeric Cauliflower Popcorn

Servings: 4
Cooking Time: 11 Minutes

Ingredients:

- 1 cup cauliflower florets
- 1 teaspoon ground turmeric
- 2 eggs, beaten
- 2 tablespoons almond flour
- 1 teaspoon salt
- Cooking spray

Directions:

1. Cut the cauliflower florets into small pieces and sprinkle with ground turmeric and salt.
2. Then dip the vegetables in the eggs and coat in the almond flour.
3. Preheat the Air Fryer to 400F.
4. Place the cauliflower popcorn in the Air Fryer in one layer and cook for 7 minutes.
5. Give a good shake to the vegetables and cook them for 4 minutes more.

Southern Cheese Straws

Servings: 6
Cooking Time: 30 Minutes

Ingredients:

- 1 cup all-purpose flour
- Sea salt and ground black pepper, to taste
- 1/4 teaspoon smoked paprika
- 1/2 teaspoon celery seeds
- 4 ounces mature Cheddar, cold, freshly grated
- 1 sticks butter

Directions:

1. Start by preheating your Air Fryer to 330 degrees F. Line the Air Fryer basket with parchment paper.
2. In a mixing bowl, thoroughly combine the flour, salt, black pepper, paprika, and celery seeds.
3. Then, combine the cheese and butter in the bowl of a stand mixer. Slowly stir in the flour mixture and mix to combine well.
4. Then, pack the dough into a cookie press fitted with a star disk. Pipe the long ribbons of dough across the parchment paper. Then cut into six-inch lengths.
5. Bake in the preheated Air Fryer for 1 minutes.
6. Repeat with the remaining dough. Let the cheese straws cool on a rack. You can store them between sheets of parchment in an airtight container.
7. Bon appétit!

Loaded Tater Tot Bites

Servings: 6
Cooking Time: 20 Minutes

Ingredients:

- 24 tater tots, frozen
- 1 cup Swiss cheese, grated
- 6 tablespoons Canadian bacon, cooked and chopped
- 1/4 cup Ranch dressing

Directions:

1. Spritz the silicone muffin cups with non-stick cooking spray. Now, press the tater tots down into each cup.
2. Divide the cheese, bacon, and Ranch dressing between tater tot cups.
3. Cook in the preheated Air Fryer at 5 degrees for 10 minutes. Serve in paper cake cups.
4. Bon appétit!

Lava Rice Bites

Servings: 4
Cooking Time: 20 Minutes

Ingredients:

- 3 cups cooked risotto
- 1/3 cup Parmesan cheese, grated
- 1 egg, beaten
- 3-ounce mozzarella cheese, cubed
- ¾ cup bread crumbs
- 1 tablespoon olive oil

Directions:

1. Preheat the Air Fryer to 390 o F and grease an Air Fryer basket.
2. Mix risotto, olive oil, Parmesan cheese and egg in a bowl until well combined.
3. Make small equal-sized balls from mixture and put a mozzarella cube in the center of each ball.
4. Smooth the risotto mixture with your finger to cover the cheese.
5. Place the bread crumbs in a shallow dish and coat the balls evenly in bread crumbs.
6. Transfer the balls into the Air Fryer basket and cook for about 10 minutes.
7. Dish out and serve warm.

Asian Teriyaki Chicken

Servings: 6
Cooking Time: 40 Minutes

Ingredients:

- 1 ½ pounds chicken drumettes
- Sea salt and cracked black pepper, to taste
- 2 tablespoons fresh chives, roughly chopped

Teriyaki Sauce:

- 1 tablespoon sesame oil
- 1/4 cup soy sauce
- 1/2 cup water
- 1/2 teaspoon Five-spice powder

- 2 tablespoons rice wine vinegar
- 1/2 teaspoon fresh ginger, grated
- 2 cloves garlic, crushed

Directions:

1. Start by preheating your Air Fryer to 380 degrees F. Rub the chicken drumettes with salt and cracked black pepper.
2. Cook in the preheated Air Fryer approximately 15 minutes. Turn them over and cook an additional 7 minutes.
3. While the chicken drumettes are roasting, combine the sesame oil, soy sauce, water, Five-spice powder, vinegar, ginger, and garlic in a pan over medium heat. Cook for 5 minutes, stirring occasionally.
4. Now, reduce the heat and let it simmer until the glaze thickens.
5. After that, brush the glaze all over the chicken drumettes. Air-fry for a further 6 minutes or until the surface is crispy. Serve topped with the remaining glaze and garnished with fresh chives.
6. Bon appétit!

Healthy Broccoli Tots

Servings: 4
Cooking Time: 25 Minutes

Ingredients:

- 1 lb broccoli, chopped
- 1/2 cup almond flour
- 1/4 cup ground flaxseed
- 1/2 tsp garlic powder
- 1 tsp salt

Directions:

1. Add broccoli into the microwave-safe bowl and microwave for 3 minutes.
2. Transfer steamed broccoli into the food processor and process until it looks like rice.
3. Transfer broccoli to a large mixing bowl.
4. Add remaining ingredients into the bowl and mix until well combined.
5. Spray Air Fryer basket with cooking spray.
6. Make small tots from broccoli mixture and place into the Air Fryer basket.
7. Cook broccoli tots for 12 minutes at 3 F.
8. Serve and enjoy.

Curly's Cauliflower

Servings: 4
Cooking Time: 30 Minutes

Ingredients:

- 4 cups bite-sized cauliflower florets
- 1 cup friendly bread crumbs, mixed with 1 tsp. salt
- ¼ cup melted butter [vegan/other]
- ¼ cup buffalo sauce [vegan/other]
- Mayo [vegan/other] or creamy dressing for dipping

Directions:

1. In a bowl, combine the butter and buffalo sauce to create a creamy paste.
2. Completely cover each floret with the sauce.
3. Coat the florets with the bread crumb mixture. Cook the florets in the Air Fryer for approximately 15 minutes at 350°F, shaking the basket occasionally.
4. Serve with a raw vegetable salad, mayo or creamy dressing.

Honey Carrots

Servings: 4
Cooking Time: 20 Minutes

Ingredients:

- 1 tbsp. honey
- 3 cups baby carrots or carrots, cut into bite-size pieces
- 1 tbsp. olive oil
- Sea salt to taste
- Ground black pepper to taste

Directions:

1. In a bowl, combine the carrots, honey, and olive oil, coating the carrots completely.
2. Sprinkle on some salt and ground black pepper.
3. Transfer the carrots to the Air Fryer and cook at 390°F for 1minutes.
4. Serve immediately.

Desserts

Spongy Cinnamon Donuts

Cooking Time: 8 Minutes

Ingredients:

- 2¼ cups plain flour
- 1½ teaspoons baking powder
- 2 large egg yolks
- 2 tablespoons butter, melted
- Salt, to taste
- ½ cup sugar
- ½ cup sour cream
- 1/3 cup caster sugar
- 1 teaspoon cinnamon

Directions:

1. Preheat the Air Fryer to 355 o F and grease an Air Fryer basket lightly.
2. Sift together flour, baking powder and salt in a large bowl.
3. Add sugar and cold butter and mix until a coarse crumb is formed.
4. Stir in the egg yolks, ½ of the sour cream and 1/3 of the flour mixture and mix until a dough is formed.
5. Add remaining sour cream and 1/3 of the flour mixture and mix until well combined.
6. Stir in the remaining flour mixture and combine well.
7. Roll the dough into ½ inch thickness onto a floured surface and cut into donuts with a donut cutter.
8. Coat butter on both sides of the donuts and arrange in the Air Fryer basket.
9. Cook for about 8 minutes until golden and sprinkle with cinnamon sugar to serve.

Cranberry Cream Surprise

Servings: 1
Cooking Time: 30 Minutes

Ingredients:

- 1 cup mashed cranberries
- ½ cup Confectioner's Style Swerve
- 2 tsp natural cherry flavoring
- 2 tsp natural rum flavoring
- 1 cup organic heavy cream

Directions:

1. Combine the mashed cranberries, sweetener, cherry and rum flavorings.
2. Cover and refrigerate for minutes.
3. Whip the heavy cream until soft peaks form.
4. Layer the whipped cream and cranberry mixture.
5. Top with fresh cranberries, mint leaves or grated dark chocolate.
6. Serve!

Baked Coconut Doughnuts

Servings: 6
Cooking Time: 20 Minutes

Ingredients:

- 1 ½ cups all-purpose flour
- 1 teaspoon baking powder
- A pinch of kosher salt
- A pinch of freshly grated nutmeg
- 1/2 cup white sugar
- 2 eggs
- 2 tablespoons full-fat coconut milk
- 2 tablespoons coconut oil, melted
- 1/4 teaspoon ground cardamom
- 1/4 teaspoon ground cinnamon
- 1 teaspoon coconut essence
- 1/2 teaspoon vanilla essence
- 1 cup coconut flakes

Directions:

1. In a mixing bowl, thoroughly combine the all-purpose flour with the baking powder, salt, nutmeg, and sugar.
2. In a separate bowl, beat the eggs until frothy using a hand mixer; add the coconut milk and oil and beat again; lastly, stir in the spices and mix again until everything is well combined.
3. Then, stir the egg mixture into the flour mixture and continue mixing until a dough ball forms. Try not to over-mix your dough. Transfer to a lightly floured surface.
4. Roll out your dough to a 1/inch thickness using a rolling pin. Cut out the doughnuts using a 3-inch round cutter; now, use a 1-inch round cutter to remove the center.

Swedish Chocolate Mug Cake

Servings: 1
Cooking Time: 15 Minutes

Ingredients:

- 1 tbsp. cocoa powder
- 3 tbsp. coconut oil
- ¼ cup flour
- 3 tbsp. whole milk
- 5 tbsp. sugar

Directions:

1. In a bowl, stir together all of the ingredients to combine them completely.
2. Take a short, stout mug and pour the mixture into it.
3. Put the mug in your Air Fryer and cook for 10 minutes at 0°F.

Nutella And Banana Pastries

Servings: 4
Cooking Time: 12 Minutes

Ingredients:

- 1 puff pastry sheet, cut into 4 equal squares
- ½ cup Nutella
- 2 bananas, sliced
- 2 tablespoons icing sugar

Directions:

1. Preheat the Air Fryer to 375 o F and grease an Air Fryer basket.
2. Spread Nutella on each pastry square and top with banana slices and icing sugar.
3. Fold each square into a triangle and slightly press the edges with a fork.
4. Arrange the pastries in the Air Fryer basket and cook for about 12 minutes.
5. Dish out and serve immediately.

Pecan Fudge Brownies

Servings: 6
Cooking Time: 30 Minutes

Ingredients:

- 1/2 cup butter, melted
- 1/2 cup sugar
- 1 teaspoon vanilla essence
- 1 egg
- 1/2 cup flour
- 1/2 teaspoon baking powder
- 1/4 cup cocoa powder
- 1/2 teaspoon ground cinnamon
- 1/4 teaspoon fine sea salt
- 1 ounce semisweet chocolate, coarsely chopped
- 1/4 cup pecans, finely chopped

Directions:

1. Start by preheating your Air Fryer to 350 degrees F. Now, lightly grease six silicone molds.
2. In a mixing dish, beat the melted butter with the sugar until fluffy. Next, stir in the vanilla and egg and beat again.
3. After that, add the flour, baking powder, cocoa powder, cinnamon, and salt. Mix until everything is well combined.
4. Fold in the chocolate and pecans; mix to combine. Bake in the preheated Air Fryer for 20 to 22 minutes.
5. Enjoy!

Pineapple Cake

Servings: 4
Cooking Time: 50 Minutes

Ingredients:

- 8 oz self-rising flour
- 4 oz butter
- 7 oz pineapple chunks
- ½ cup pineapple juice
- 1 egg
- 2 tbsp milk
- ½ cup sugar

Directions:

1. Preheat the Air Fryer to 390 F, place the butter and flour into a bowl, and rub the mixture with your fingers until crumbed.
2. Stir in pineapple, sugar, chocolate, and juice.
3. Beat eggs and milk separately, and then add to the batter.
4. Transfer the batter to a previously prepared (greased or lined) cake pan, and cook for 40 minutes.
5. Let cool for at least minutes before serving.

Flavor-Packed Clafoutis

Servings: 4
Cooking Time: 25 Minutes

Ingredients:

- 1½ cups fresh cherries, pitted
- ¼ cup flour
- 1 egg
- 1 tablespoon butter
- 3 tablespoons vodka
- 2 tablespoons sugar
- Pinch of salt
- ½ cup sour cream
- ¼ cup powdered sugar

Directions:

1. Preheat the Air Fryer to 355 o F and grease a baking pan lightly.
2. Mix cherries and vodka in a bowl.
3. Sift together flour, sugar and salt in another bowl.
4. Stir in the sour cream and egg until a smooth dough is formed.
5. Transfer the dough evenly into the baking pan and top with the cherry mixture and butter.
6. Place the baking pan in the Air Fryer basket and cook for about 25 minutes.
7. Dust with powdered sugar and serve warm.

Coconut Sunflower Cookies

Servings: 8
Cooking Time: 10 Minutes

Ingredients:

- 5 oz sunflower seed butter
- 6 tbsp coconut flour
- 1 tsp vanilla
- ¼ tsp olive oil
- 2 tbsp swerve
- Pinch of salt

Directions:

1. Add all ingredients into the bowl and mix until dough is formed.
2. Preheat the Air Fryer to 360 F.
3. Make cookies from mixture and place into the Air Fryer and cook for 10 minutes.
4. Serve and enjoy.

Almond Pumpkin Cookies

Servings: 8
Cooking Time: 8 Minutes

Ingredients:

- ¼ cup almond flour
- ½ cup pumpkin puree
- 3 tbsp swerve
- ½ tsp baking soda
- 1 tbsp coconut flakes
- ½ tsp cinnamon
- Pinch of salt

Directions:

1. Preheat the Air Fryer to 360 F.
2. Add all ingredients into the bowl and mix until well combined.
3. Spray Air Fryer basket with cooking spray.
4. Make cookies from bowl mixture and place into the Air Fryer and cook for 8 minutes.
5. Serve and enjoy.

Peach Parcel

Servings: 2
Cooking Time: 15 Minutes

Ingredients:

- 1 peach, peeled, cored and halved
- 1 cup prepared vanilla custard
- 2 puff pastry sheets
- 1 egg, beaten lightly
- 1 tablespoon sugar
- Pinch of ground cinnamon
- 1 tablespoon whipped cream

Directions:

1. Preheat the Air Fryer to 340 o F and grease an Air Fryer basket.
2. Place a spoonful of vanilla custard and a peach half in the center of each pastry sheet.
3. Mix sugar and cinnamon in a bowl and sprinkle on the peach halves.
4. Pinch the corners of sheets together to shape into a parcel and transfer into the Air Fryer basket.
5. Cook for about 1 minutes and top with whipped cream.
6. Dish out and serve with remaining custard.

Ginger Vanilla Cookies

Servings: 12
Cooking Time: 15 Minutes

Ingredients:

- 2 cups almond flour
- 1 cup swerve
- ¼ cup butter, melted
- 1 egg
- 2 teaspoons ginger, grated
- 1 teaspoon vanilla extract
- ¼ teaspoon nutmeg, ground
- ¼ teaspoon cinnamon powder

Directions:

1. In a bowl, mix all the ingredients and whisk well.
2. Spoon small balls out of this mix on a lined baking sheet that fits the Air Fryer lined with parchment paper and flatten them.
3. Put the sheet in the Fryer and cook at 360 degrees F for minutes.
4. Cool the cookies down and serve.

Yummy Banana Cookies

Servings: 6
Cooking Time: 10 Minutes

Ingredients:

- 1 cup dates, pitted and chopped
- 1 teaspoon vanilla
- 1/3 cup vegetable oil
- 2 cups rolled oats
- 3 ripe bananas

Directions:

1. Preheat the Air Fryer to 3500F.
2. In a bowl, mash the bananas and add in the rest of the ingredients.
3. Let it rest inside the fridge for 10 minutes.
4. Drop a teaspoonful on cut parchment paper.
5. Place the cookies on parchment paper inside the air fryer basket. Make sure that the cookies do not overlap.
6. Cook for 20 minutes or until the edges are crispy.
7. Serve with almond milk.

Berry Layer Cake

Servings: 1
Cooking Time: 8 Minutes

Ingredients:

- ¼ lemon pound cake
- ¼ cup whipping cream
- ½ tsp Truvia
- 1/8 tsp orange flavor
- 1 cup of mixed berries

Directions:

1. Using a sharp knife, divide the lemon cake into small cubes.
2. Dice the strawberries.
3. Combine the whipping cream, Truvia, and orange flavor.
4. Layer the fruit, cake and cream in a glass.
5. Serve!

Cardamom Coconut Cookies

Servings: 6
Cooking Time: 10 Minutes

Ingredients:

- 3 tablespoons coconut oil, softened
- 4 tablespoons coconut flour
- 2 tablespoons flax meal
- 2 tablespoons Monk fruit
- 1 teaspoon poppy seeds
- ½ teaspoon baking powder
- ½ teaspoon lemon juice
- ¼ teaspoon ground cardamom
- Cooking spray

Directions:

1. In the mixing bowl put coconut oil, coconut flour, flax meal, ad Monk fruit.
2. Then add poppy seeds, baking powder, lemon juice, and cardamom.
3. With the help of the fingertips knead the soft but non-sticky dough.
4. Then make the cookies from the dough.
5. Preheat the Air Fryer to 375F. Spray the Air Fryer basket with cooking spray.
6. Place the cookies in the Air Fryer and cook them for minutes.
7.

Orange Galettes

Servings: 6
Cooking Time: 15 Minutes

Ingredients:

- 1 cup almond meal
- 1/2 cup coconut flour
- 3 eggs
- 1/3 cup milk
- 2 tablespoons monk fruit
- 2 teaspoons grated lemon peel
- 1/3 teaspoon ground nutmeg, preferably freshly ground
- 1 ½ teaspoons baking powder
- 3 tablespoons orange juice
- A pinch of turmeric

Directions:

1. Grab two mixing bowls. Combine dry ingredients in the first bowl.
2. In the second bowl, combine all wet ingredients. Add wet mixture to the dry mixture and mix until smooth and uniform.
3. Air-fry for 4 to 5 minutes at 5 degrees F. Work in batches.
4. Dust with confectioners' swerve if desired. Bon appétit!

Creamy Crumble

Servings: 4
Cooking Time: 20 Minutes

Ingredients:

- 4 oz rhubarb, chopped
- ¼ cup heavy cream
- 1 teaspoon ground cinnamon
- ¼ cup Erythritol
- 1 cup almond flour
- 1 egg, beaten
- 1 teaspoon avocado oil
- 4 teaspoons butter, softened

Directions:

1. In the bowl mix up heavy cream, ground cinnamon, almond flour, egg, and butter. Stir the mixture until you get the crumbly texture.
2. Then mix up rhubarb and Erythritol.
3. Brush the Air Fryer mold with avocado oil.
4. Separate the crumbled dough on 4 parts.
5. Put part of the dough in the Air Fryer mold.
6. Then sprinkle it with a small amount rhubarb.
7. Repeat the same steps till you use all ingredients.
8. Put the crumble in the Air Fryer. Cook it at 375F for 20 minutes.
9.

Chocolate Molten Lava Cake

Servings: 4
Cooking Time: 25 Minutes

Ingredients:

- 3 ½ oz. butter, melted
- 3 ½ tbsp. sugar
- 3 ½ oz. chocolate, melted
- 1 ½ tbsp. flour
- 2 eggs

Directions:

1. Pre-heat the Air Fryer to 375°F.
2. Grease four ramekins with a little butter.
3. Rigorously combine the eggs and butter before stirring in the melted chocolate.
4. Slowly fold in the flour.
5. Spoon an equal amount of the mixture into each ramekin.
6. Put them in the Air Fryer and cook for 10 minutes
7. Place the ramekins upside-down on plates and let the cakes fall out. Serve hot.

Rhubarb Pie Recipe

Servings: 6
Cooking Time: 1 Hour 15 Minutes

Ingredients:

- 1 ¼ cups almond flour
- 5 tbsp. cold water
- 8 tbsp. butter
- 1 tsp. sugar For the filling:
- 3 cups rhubarb; chopped.
- 1/2 tsp. nutmeg; ground
- 1 tbsp. butter
- 3 tbsp. flour
- 1 ½ cups sugar
- 2 eggs
- 2 tbsp. low fat milk

Directions:

1. In a bowl; mix ¼ cups flour with 1 tsp. sugar, 8 tbsp. butter and cold water; stir and knead until you obtain a dough.
2. Transfer dough to a floured working surface, shape a disk, flatten, wrap in plastic, keep in the fridge for about 30 minutes; roll and press on the bottom of a pie pan that fits your Air Fryer.
3. In a bowl; mix rhubarb with 1 ½ cups sugar, nutmeg, tbsp. flour and whisk.
4. In another bowl, whisk eggs with milk, add to rhubarb mix, pour the whole mix into the pie crust, introduce in your Air Fryer and cook at 390 °F, for minutes.
5. Cut and serve it cold.

No Flour Lime Muffins

Servings: 6
Cooking Time: 30 Minutes

Ingredients:

- Juice and zest of 2 limes
- 1 cup yogurt
- ¼ cup superfine sugar
- 8 oz cream cheese
- 1 tsp vanilla extract

Directions:

1. Preheat the Air Fryer to 330 F, and with a spatula, gently combine the yogurt and cheese.
2. In another bowl, beat together the rest of the ingredients.
3. Gently fold the lime with the cheese mixture.
4. Divide the batter between 6 lined muffin tins.
5. Cook in the Air Fryer for minutes.

Raspberry Pudding Surprise

Servings: 1
Cooking Time: 40 Minutes

Ingredients:

- 3 tbsp chia seeds
- ½ cup unsweetened milk
- 1 scoop chocolate protein powder
- ¼ cup raspberries, fresh or frozen
- 1 tsp honey

Directions:

1. Combine the milk, protein powder and chia seeds together.
2. Let rest for 5 minutes before stirring.
3. Refrigerate for minutes.
4. Top with raspberries.
5. Serve!

Cream Cups

Servings: 6
Cooking Time: 10 Minutes

Ingredients:

- 2 tablespoons butter, melted
- 8 ounces cream cheese, soft
- 3 tablespoons coconut, shredded and unsweetened
- 3 eggs
- 4 tablespoons swerve

Directions:

1. In a bowl, mix all the ingredients and whisk really well.
2. Divide into small ramekins, put them in the fryer and cook at 320 degrees F and bake for minutes.
3. Serve cold.

Picnic Blackberry Muffins

Servings: 8
Cooking Time: 20 Minutes

Ingredients:

- 1 ½ cups almond flour
- 1/2 teaspoon baking soda
- 1 teaspoon baking powder
- 1/4 teaspoon kosher salt
- 1/2 cup swerve
- 2 eggs, whisked
- 1/2 cup milk
- 1/4 cup coconut oil, melted
- 1/2 teaspoon vanilla paste
- 1/2 cup fresh blackberries

Directions:

1. In a mixing bowl, combine the almond flour, baking soda, baking powder, swerve, and salt. Whisk to combine well.
2. In another mixing bowl, mix the eggs, milk, coconut oil, and vanilla.
3. Now, add the wet egg mixture to dry the flour mixture. Then, carefully fold in the fresh blackberries; gently stir to combine.
4. Scrape the batter mixture into the muffin cups. Bake your muffins at 350 degrees F for 12 minutes or until the tops are golden brown.
5. Sprinkle some extra icing sugar over the top of each muffin if desired.
6. Serve and enjoy!

Semolina Cake

Servings: 8
Cooking Time: 15 Minutes

Ingredients:

- 2½ cups semolina
- 1 cup milk
- 1 cup Greek yogurt
- 2 teaspoons baking powder
- ½ cup walnuts, chopped
- ½ cup vegetable oil
- 1 cup sugar
- Pinch of salt

Directions:

1. Preheat the Air Fryer to 360 o F and grease a baking pan lightly.
2. Mix semolina, oil, milk, yogurt and sugar in a bowl until well combined.
3. Cover the bowl and keep aside for about 15 minutes.
4. Stir in the baking soda, baking powder and salt and fold in the walnuts.
5. Transfer the mixture into the baking pan and place in the Air Fryer.
6. Cook for about 15 minutes and dish out to serve.

Chocolate Chip In A Mug

Servings: 6
Cooking Time: 20 Minutes

Ingredients:

- ¼ cup walnuts, shelled and chopped
- ½ cup butter, unsalted
- ½ cup dark chocolate chips
- ½ cup erythritol
- ½ teaspoon baking soda
- ½ teaspoon salt
- 1 tablespoon vanilla extract
- 2 ½ cups almond flour
- 2 large eggs, beaten

Directions:

1. Preheat the Air Fryer for 5 minutes.
2. Combine all ingredients in a mixing bowl.
3. Place in greased mugs.
4. Bake in the Air Fryer for 20 minutes at 3750F.

Creamy Nutmeg Cake

Servings: 8
Cooking Time: 40 Minutes

Ingredients:

- ½ cup heavy cream
- 3 eggs, beaten
- 3 tablespoons cocoa powder
- 1 teaspoon vanilla extract
- 1 teaspoon baking powder
- 3 tablespoons Erythritol
- 1 cup almond flour
- ¼ teaspoon ground nutmeg
- 1 tablespoon avocado oil
- 1 teaspoon Splenda

Directions:

1. Mix up heavy cream and eggs in the bowl. Add cocoa powder and stir the liquid until it is smooth.
2. After this, add vanilla extract, baking powder, Erythritol, almond flour, ground nutmeg, and avocado oil. Whisk the mixture gently and pour it in the cake mold.
3. Then cover the cake with foil. Secure the edges of the foil.
4. Then pierce the foil with the help of the toothpick.
5. Preheat the Air Fryer to 360F. Put the cake mold in the Air Fryer and cook it for 40 minutes. When the cake is cooked, remove it from the Air Fryer and cool completely.
6. Remove the cake from the mold and them sprinkle with Splenda.

Apple Dumplings

Servings: 2
Cooking Time: 40 Minutes

Ingredients:

- 2 tbsp. sultanas
- 2 sheets puff pastry
- 2 tbsp. butter, melted
- 2 small apples
- 1 tbsp. sugar

Directions:

1. Pre-heat your Air Fryer to 350°F.
2. Peel the apples and remove the cores.
3. In a bowl, stir together the sugar and the sultanas.
4. Lay one apple on top of each pastry sheet and stuff the sugar and sultanas into the holes where the cores used to be.
5. Wrap the pastry around the apples, covering them completely.
6. Put them on a sheet of aluminum foil and coat each dumpling with a light brushing of melted butter.
7. Transfer to the Air Fryer and bake for 25 minutes until a golden brown color is achieved and the apples have softened inside.

Coconutty Lemon Bars

Servings: 12
Cooking Time: 25 Minutes

Ingredients:

- ¼ cup cashew
- ¼ cup fresh lemon juice, freshly squeezed
- ¾ cup coconut milk
- ¾ cup erythritol
- 1 cup desiccated coconut
- 1 teaspoon baking powder
- 2 eggs, beaten
- 2 tablespoons coconut oil
- A dash of salt

Directions:

1. Preheat the Air Fryer for 5 minutes.
2. In a mixing bowl, combine all ingredients.
3. Use a hand mixer to mix everything.
4. Pour into a baking dish that will fit in the air fryer.
5. Bake for 2 minutes at 3500F or until a toothpick inserted in the middle comes out clean.

Raspberry Coconut Cupcake

Servings: 6
Cooking Time: 30 Minutes

Ingredients:

- ½ cup butter
- ½ teaspoon salt
- ¾ cup erythritol
- 1 cup almond milk, unsweetened
- 1 cup coconut flour
- 1 tablespoon baking powder
- 3 teaspoons vanilla extract
- 7 large eggs, beaten

Directions:

1. Preheat the Air Fryer for 5 minutes.
2. Mix all ingredients using a hand mixer.
3. Pour into hard cupcake molds.
4. Place in the Air Fryer basket.
5. Bake for 30 minutes at 30F or until a toothpick inserted in the middle comes out clean.
6. Bake by batches if possible.
7. Allow to chill before serving.

Air Fried Snickerdoodle Poppers

Servings: 6
Cooking Time: 30 Minutes

Ingredients:

- 1 can of Pillsbury Grands Flaky Layers Biscuits
- 1 ½ cups cinnamon sugar
- melted butter, for brushing

Directions:

1. Preheat Air Fryer to 350 F.
2. Unroll the flaky biscuits; cut them into fourths. Roll each ¼ into a ball.
3. Arrange the balls on a lined baking sheet, and cook in the Air Fryer for 7 minutes, or until golden.
4. Prepare the Jell-O following the package's instructions.
5. Using an injector, inject some of the vanilla pudding into each ball.
6. Brush the balls with melted butter and then coat them with cinnamon sugar.

Banana Crepes With Apple Topping

Servings: 2
Cooking Time: 40 Minutes

Ingredients:

Banana Crepes:
- 1 large banana, mashed
- 2 eggs, beaten
- 1/4 teaspoon baking powder
- 1 shot dark rum
- 1/2 teaspoon vanilla extract
- 1 teaspoon butter, melted
- 2 tablespoons brown sugar

Topping:
- 2 apples, peeled, cored, and chopped
- 2 tablespoons sugar
- 1/2 teaspoon cinnamon
- 3 tablespoons water

Directions:

1. Mix all ingredients for the banana crepes until creamy and fluffy. Let it stand for to 20 minutes.
2. Spritz the Air Fryer baking pan with cooking spray. Pour the batter into the pan using a measuring cup.
3. Cook at 2 degrees F for 4 to 5 minutes or until golden brown.
4. Repeat with the remaining batter.
5. To make the pancake topping, place all ingredients in a heavy- bottomed skillet over medium heat. Cook for 10 minutes, stirring occasionally.
6. Spoon on top of the banana crepes and enjoy!

Chocolate Brownie

Servings: 4
Cooking Time: 16 Minutes

Ingredients:

- 1 cup bananas, overripe
- 1 scoop protein powder
- 2 tbsp unsweetened cocoa powder
- 1/2 cup almond butter, melted

Directions:

1. Preheat the Air Fryer to 325 F.
2. Spray Air Fryer baking pan with cooking spray.
3. Add all ingredients into the blender and blend until smooth.
4. Pour batter into the prepared pan and place in the Air Fryer basket.
5. Cook brownie for 16 minutes.
6. Serve and enjoy.

White Chocolate Rum Molten Cake

Servings: 4
Cooking Time: 20 Minutes

Ingredients:

- 2 ½ ounces butter, at room temperature
- 3 ounces white chocolate
- 2 eggs, beaten
- 1/2 cup powdered sugar
- 1/3 cup self-rising flour
- 1 teaspoon rum extract
- 1 teaspoon vanilla extract

Directions:

1. Begin by preheating your Air Fryer to 370 degrees F. Spritz the sides and bottom of four ramekins with cooking spray.
2. Melt the butter and white chocolate in a microwave-safe bowl. Mix the eggs and sugar until frothy.
3. Pour the butter/chocolate mixture into the egg mixture. Stir in the flour, rum extract, and vanilla extract. Mix until everything is well incorporated.
4. Scrape the batter into the prepared ramekins. Bake in the preheated Air Fryer for 9 to 11 minutes.
5. Let stand for 2 to 3 minutes. Invert on a plate while warm and serve. Bon appétit!

The Most Chocolaty Fudge

Servings: 6
Cooking Time: 55 Minutes

Ingredients:

- 7 oz flour
- 1 tbsp honey
- ¼ cup milk
- 1 tsp vanilla extract
- 1 oz cocoa powder
- 2 eggs
- 4 oz butter
- 1 orange, juice and zest Icing:
- 1 oz butter, melted
- 4 oz powdered sugar
- 1 tbsp brown sugar
- 1 tbsp milk
- 2 tsp honey

Directions:

1. Preheat Air Fryer to 350 F, and in a bowl, mix the dry ingredients for the fudge.
2. Mix the wet ingredients separately; combine the two mixtures.
3. Transfer the batter to a prepared cake pan.
4. Cook for 35 minutes.
5. Whisk together all icing ingredients.
6. When the cake cools, coat with the icing.
7. Let set before slicing.

209

Apple Caramel Relish

Servings: 4
Cooking Time: 40 Minutes

Ingredients:

- 2 apples, peeled, sliced
- 3 oz butter, melted
- ½ cup brown sugar
- 1 tsp cinnamon
- ½ cup flour
- 1 cup caramel sauce

Directions:

1. Line a cake tin with baking paper.
2. In a bowl, mix butter, sugar, cinnamon and flour until you obtain a crumbly texture.
3. Prepare the cake mix according to the instructions (no baking).
4. Pour the batter into the tin and arrange the apple slices on top.
5. Spoon the caramel over the apples and add the crumble over the sauce.
6. Cook in the Air Fryer for 35 minutes at 360 F; make sure to check it halfway through, so it's not overcooked.

Lemon Berry Jam

Servings: 12
Cooking Time: 20 Minutes

Ingredients:

- ¼ cup swerve
- 8 ounces strawberries, sliced
- 1 tablespoon lemon juice
- ¼ cup water

Directions:

1. In a pan that fits the Air Fryer, combine all the ingredients, put the pan in the machine and cook at 380 degrees F for 20 minutes.
2. Divide the mix into cups, cool down and serve.

Cinnamon And Sugar Sweet Potato Fries

Servings: 2
Cooking Time: 30 Minutes

Ingredients:

- 1 large sweet potato, peeled and sliced into sticks
- 1 teaspoon ghee
- 1 tablespoon cornstarch
- 1/4 teaspoon ground cardamom
- 1/4 cup sugar
- 1 tablespoon ground cinnamon

Directions:

1. Toss the sweet potato sticks with the melted ghee and cornstarch.
2. Cook in the preheated Air Fryer at 380 degrees F for minutes, shaking the basket halfway through the cooking time.
3. Sprinkle the cardamom, sugar, and cinnamon all over the sweet potato fries and serve.
4. Bon appétit!

Sour Cream Blueberry Coffee Cake

Servings: 6
Cooking Time: 35 Minutes

Ingredients:

- 1/2 cup butter, softened
- 1 cup white sugar
- 1 egg
- 1/2 cup sour cream
- 1/2 teaspoon vanilla extract
- 3/4 cup and
- 1 tablespoon all-purpose flour

- 1/2 teaspoon baking powder
- 1/8 teaspoon salt
- 1/2 cup fresh or frozen blueberries
- 1/4 cup brown sugar
- 1/2 teaspoon ground cinnamon
- 1/4 cup chopped pecans
- 1-1 /2 teaspoons confectioners' sugar for dusting

Directions:

1. In a small bowl, whisk well pecans, cinnamon, and brown sugar.
2. In a blender, blend well all wet Ingredients. Add dry Ingredients: except for confectioner's sugar and blueberries. Blend well until smooth and creamy.
3. Lightly grease baking pan of air fryer with cooking spray.
4. Pour half of batter in pan. Sprinkle half of pecan mixture on top. Pour the remaining batter. And then topped with remaining pecan mixture.
5. Cover pan with foil.
6. For 35 minutes, cook on 330oF.
7. Serve and enjoy with a dusting of confectioner's sugar.

Avocado Pudding

Servings: 1
Cooking Time: 5 Minutes

Ingredients:

- Avocado
- 3 tsp. liquid Sugar
- 1 tbsp. cocoa powder
- 4 tsp. unsweetened milk
- ¼ tsp. vanilla extract

Directions:

1. Pre-heat your Fryer at 360°F.
2. Halve the avocado, twist to open, and scoop out the pit.
3. Spoon the flesh into a bowl and mash it with a fork. Throw in the Sugar, cocoa powder, milk, and vanilla extract, and combine everything with a hand mixer.
4. Transfer this mixture to the basket of your fryer and cook for three minutes.

Chocolate Rum Lava Cake

Servings: 4
Cooking Time: 20 Minutes

Ingredients:

- 2 ½ ounces butter, at room temperature
- 3 ounces chocolate, unsweetened
- 2 eggs, beaten
- 1/2 cup confectioners' swerve
- 1/2 cup almond flour
- 1 teaspoon rum extract
- 1 teaspoon vanilla extract

Directions:

1. Begin by preheating your Air Fryer to 370 degrees F. Spritz the sides and bottom of four ramekins with cooking spray.
2. Melt the butter and chocolate in a microwave-safe bowl. Mix the eggs and confectioners' swerve until frothy.
3. Pour the butter/chocolate mixture into the egg mixture. Stir in the almond flour, rum extract, and vanilla extract. Mix until everything is well incorporated.
4. Scrape the batter into the prepared ramekins. Bake in the preheated Air Fryer for 9 to 11 minutes.
5. Let stand for 2 to 3 minutes. Invert on a plate while warm and serve. Bon appétit!

Espresso Brownies With Mascarpone Frosting

Servings: 8
Cooking Time: 40 Minutes

Ingredients:

- 5 ounces unsweetened chocolate, chopped into chunks
- 2 tablespoons instant espresso powder
- 1 tablespoon cocoa powder, unsweetened
- 1/2 cup almond butter
- 1/2 cup almond meal
- 3/4 cup swerve
- 1   teaspoon pure coffee extract
- 1/2 teaspoon lime peel zest
- 1/4 cup coconut flour
- 2   eggs plus
- 1 egg yolk

- 1/2 teaspoon baking soda
- 1/2 teaspoon baking powder
- 1/2 teaspoon ground cinnamon
- 1/3 teaspoon ancho chile powder

For the Chocolate Mascarpone Frosting:
- 4 ounces mascarpone cheese, at room temperature
- 1 ½ ounces unsweetened chocolate chips
- 1 ½ cups confectioner's swerve
- 1/4 cup unsalted butter, at room temperature
- 1 teaspoon vanilla paste
- A pinch of fine sea salt

Directions:

1. First of all, microwave the chocolate and almond butter until completely melted; allow the mixture to cool at room temperature.
2. Then, whisk the eggs, swerve, cinnamon, espresso powder, coffee extract, ancho chile powder, and lime zest.
3. Next step, add the vanilla/egg mixture to the chocolate/butter mixture. Stir in the almond meal and coconut flour along with baking soda, baking powder and cocoa powder.
4. Finally, press the batter into a lightly buttered cake pan. Air-fry for 35 minutes at 3 degrees F.
5. In the meantime, make the frosting. Beat the butter and mascarpone cheese until creamy. Add in the melted chocolate chips and vanilla paste.
6. Gradually, stir in the confectioner's swerve and salt; beat untileverything's well combined. Lastly, frost the brownies and serve.

Cardamom Bombs

Servings: 2
Cooking Time: 5 Minutes

Ingredients:

- 2 oz avocado, peeled
- 1 egg, beaten
- ½ teaspoon ground cardamom
- 1 tablespoon Erythritol
- 2 tablespoons coconut flour
- 1 teaspoon butter, softened

Directions:

1. Put the avocado in the bowl and mash it with the help of the fork. Add egg and stir the mixture until it is smooth.
2. Then add ground cardamom, Erythritol, and coconut flour.
3. After this, add butter and stir the mixture well. Make the balls from the avocado mixture and press them gently.
4. Then preheat the Air Fryer to 400F. Put the avocado bombs in the Air Fryer and cook them for 5 minutes.

Vanilla Orange Custard

Servings: 6

Cooking Time: 35 Minutes + Chilling Time

Ingredients:

- 6 eggs
- 7 ounces cream cheese, at room temperature
- 2 ½ cans condensed milk, sweetened
- 1/2 cup swerve
- 1/2 teaspoon orange rind, grated
- 1 ½ cardamom pods, bruised
- 2 teaspoons vanilla paste
- 1/4 cup fresh orange juice

Directions:

1. In a saucepan, melt swerve over a moderate flame; it takes about to 12 minutes. Immediately but carefully pour the melted sugar into six ramekins, tilting to coat their bottoms; allow them to cool slightly.
2. In a mixing dish, beat the cheese until smooth; now, fold in the eggs, one at a time, and continue to beat until pale and creamy.
3. Add the orange rind, cardamom, vanilla, orange juice, and the milk; mix again. Pour the mixture over the caramelized sugar. Air- fry, covered, at 5 degrees F for 28 minutes or until it has thickened.
4. Refrigerate overnight; garnish with berries or other fruits and serve.

Passion Fruit Pudding Recipe

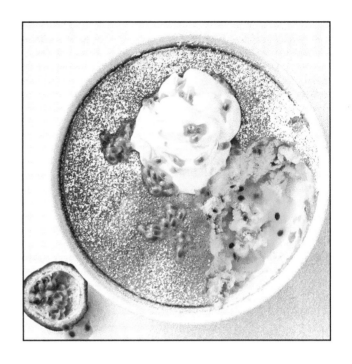

Servings: 6
Cooking Time: 50 Minutes

Ingredients:

- 1 cup Paleo passion fruit curd
- 3 ½ oz. almond milk
- 1/2 cup almond flour
- 4 passion fruits; pulp and seeds
- 3 ½ oz. maple syrup
- 3 eggs
- 2 oz. ghee; melted
- 1/2 tsp. baking powder

Directions:

1. In a bowl; mix the half of the fruit curd with passion fruit seeds and pulp; stir and divide into 6 heat proof ramekins.
2. In a bowl; whisked eggs with maple syrup, ghee, the rest of the curd, baking powder, milk and flour and stir well.
3. Divide this into the ramekins as well, introduce in the fryer and cook at 200 °F, for 40 minutes. Leave puddings to cool down and serve!

Tangerine Cake Recipe

Servings: 8
Cooking Time: 30 Minutes

Ingredients:

- 3/4 cup sugar
- 2 cups flour
- 1/2 tsp. vanilla extract
- 1/4 cup olive oil
- 1/2 cup milk
- 1 tsp. cider vinegar
- Juice and zest from
- 2 lemons Juice and zest from 1 tangerine
- Tangerine segments; for serving

Directions:

1. In a bowl; mix flour with sugar and stir.
2. In another bowl, mix oil with milk, vinegar, vanilla extract, lemon juice and zest and tangerine zest and whisk very well.
3. Add flour; stir well, pour this into a cake pan that fits your Air Fryer, introduce in the Fryer and cook at 0 °F, for 20 minutes. Serve right away with tangerine segments on top.

Raspberry Pop-Tarts

Servings: 5
Cooking Time: 10 Minutes

Ingredients:

- 2 oz raspberries
- ½ cup almond flour
- 1 egg, beaten
- 1 tablespoon butter, softened
- 1 tablespoon Erythritol
- ½ teaspoon baking powder
- 1 egg white, whisked
- Cooking spray

Directions:

1. In the mixing bowl mix up almond flour, egg, butter, and baking powder Knead the soft non-sticky dough.
2. Then mash the raspberries and mix them up with Erythritol.
3. Cut the dough into halves.
4. Then roll up every dough half into the big squares.
5. After this, cut every square into 5 small squares. Put the mashed raspberry mixture on 5 mini squares.
6. Then cover them with remaining dough squares. Secure the edges with the help of the fork.
7. Then brush the pop-tarts with whisked egg white.
8. Preheat the Air Fryer to 350F. Spray the Air Fryer basket with cooking spray.
9. Then place the pop tarts in the Air Fryer basket in one layer. Cook them at 350F for minutes.
10. Cool the cooked pop-tarts totally and transfer in the serving plates.

Lemon Pie

Servings: 8
Cooking Time: 35 Minutes

Ingredients:

- 2 eggs, whisked
- ¾ cup swerve
- ¼ cup coconut flour
- 2 tablespoons butter, melted
- 1 teaspoon lemon zest, grated
- 1 teaspoon baking powder
- 1 teaspoon vanilla extract
- ½ teaspoon lemon extract
- 4 ounces coconut, shredded
- Cooking spray

Directions:

1. In a bowl, combine all the ingredients except the cooking spray and stir well.
2. Grease a pie pan that fits the Air Fryer with the cooking spray, pour the mixture inside, put the pan in the Air Fryer and cook at 360 degrees F for 35 minutes.
3. Slice and serve warm.

Crispy Good Peaches

Servings: 4
Cooking Time: 30 Minutes

Ingredients:

- 1 teaspoon cinnamon
- 1 teaspoon sugar, white
- 1/3 cup oats, dry rolled
- 1/4 cup Flour, white
- 2 tablespoon Flour, white
- 3 tablespoon butter, unsalted
- 3 tablespoon sugar
- 3 tablespoon pecans, chopped
- 4 cup sliced peaches, frozen

Directions:

1. Lightly grease baking pan of Air Fryer with cooking spray. Mix in a tsp cinnamon, 2 tbsp flour, 3 tbsp sugar, and peaches.
2. For minutes, cook on 300oF.
3. Mix the rest of the Ingredients in a bowl. Pour over peaches.
4. Cook for 10 minutes at 330oF.
5. Serve and enjoy.

Chocolate Cake

Servings: 4
Cooking Time: 40 Minutes

Ingredients:

For Cake:
- 1/3 cup plain flour
- ¼ teaspoon baking powder
- 1½ tablespoons unsweetened cocoa powder
- 2 egg yolks
- ½ ounce caster sugar
- 2 tablespoons vegetable oil
- 3 ¾ tablespoons milk
- 1 teaspoon vanilla extract

For Meringue:
- 2 egg whites
- 1 ounce caster sugar
- 1/8 teaspoon cream of tartar

Directions:
1. For cake: in a bowl, sift together the flour, baking powder, and cocoa powder.
2. In another bowl, add the remaining ingredients and whisk until well combined.
3. Add the flour mixture and whisk until well combined.
4. For meringue: in a clean glass bowl, add all the ingredients and with an electric whisker, whisk on high speed until stiff peaks form.
5. Place 1/3 of the meringue into flour mixture and with a hand whisker, whisk well.
6. Fold in the remaining meringue.
7. Set the temperature of air fryer to 355 degrees F.
8. Place the mixture into an ungreased chiffon pan.
9. With a piece of foil, cover the pan tightly and poke some holes using a fork.
10. Arrange the cake pan into an air fryer basket.
11. Now, set the temperature of air fryer to 320 degrees F.
12. Air fry for about 30-35 minutes.
13. Remove the piece of foil and set the temperature to 285 degrees F.
14. Air fry for another 5 minutes or until a toothpick inserted in the center comes out clean.
15. Remove the cake pan from air fryer and place onto a wire rack to cool for about 10 minutes.
16. Now, invert the cake onto wire rack to completely cool before slicing.
17. Cut the cake into desired size slices and serve.

Ricotta And Lemon Cake Recipe

Servings: 4
Cooking Time: 1 Hour And 10 Minutes

Ingredients:

- 8 eggs; whisked
- 3 lbs. ricotta cheese
- Zest from 1 lemon; grated
- Zest from 1 orange; grated
- 1/2 lb. sugar
- Butter for the pan

Directions:

1. In a bowl; mix eggs with sugar, cheese, lemon and orange zest and stir very well.
2. Grease a baking pan that fits your air fryer with some batter, spread ricotta mixture, introduce in the fryer at 390 °F and bake for 30 minutes.
3. Reduce heat at 0 °F and bake for 40 more minutes. Take out of the oven, leave cake to cool down and serve!

Beef, Pork and Lamb

Teriyaki Steak With Fresh Herbs

Servings: 4
Cooking Time: 40 Minutes

Ingredients:

- 2 heaping tablespoons fresh parsley, roughly chopped
- 1 pound beef rump steaks
- 2 heaping tablespoons fresh chives, roughly chopped
- Salt and black pepper (or mixed peppercorns), to savor

For the Sauce:

- 1/4 cup rice vinegar
- 1 tablespoon fresh ginger, grated
- 1 ½ tablespoons mirin
- 3 garlic cloves, minced

- 2 tablespoon rice bran oil
- 1/3 cup soy sauce
- A few drops of liquid Stevia

Directions:

1. Firstly, steam the beef rump steaks for 8 minutes (use the method of steaming that you prefer). Season the beef with salt and black pepper; scatter the chopped parsley and chives over the top.
2. Roast the beef rump steaks in an Air Fryer basket for minutes at 345 degrees, turning halfway through.
3. While the beef is cooking, combine the ingredients for the teriyaki sauce in a sauté pan. Then, let it simmer over low heat until it has thickened.
4. Toss the beef with the teriyaki sauce until it is well covered and serve. Enjoy!

Stuffed Bell Pepper

Servings: 4
Cooking Time: 25 Minutes

Ingredients:

- 4 bell peppers, cut top of bell pepper
- 16 oz. ground beef
- 2/3 cup cheese, shredded
- ½ cup rice, cooked
- 1 tsp. basil, dried
- ½ tsp. chili powder
- 1 tsp. black pepper
- 1 tsp. garlic salt
- 2 tsp. Worcestershire sauce

- 8 oz. tomato sauce
- 2 garlic cloves, minced
- 1 small onion, chopped

Directions:

1. Grease a frying pan with cooking spray and fry the onion and garlic over a medium heat.
2. Stir in the beef, basil, chili powder, black pepper, and garlic salt, combining everything well. Allow to cook until the beef is nicely browned, before taking the pan off the heat.
3. Add in half of the cheese, the rice, Worcestershire sauce, and tomato sauce and stir to combine.
4. Spoon equal amounts of the beef mixture into the four bell peppers, filling them entirely.
5. Pre-heat the Air Fryer at 400°F.
6. Spritz the Air Fryer basket with cooking spray.
7. Put the stuffed bell peppers in the basket and allow to cook for 11 minutes.
8. Add the remaining cheese on top of each bell pepper with remaining cheese and cook for a further 2 minutes. When the cheese is melted and the bell peppers are piping hot, serve immediately. Serve hot.

Cilantro Beef Meatballs

Servings: 4
Cooking Time: 7 Minutes

Ingredients:

- 1 cup ground beef
- 3 oz Cheddar cheese, shredded
- 1 tablespoons flax meal
- 1 teaspoon fresh cilantro, chopped
- 1 garlic clove, diced
- 1 chili pepper, chopped
- 1 egg, beaten
- 1 teaspoon ground coriander
- ¼ cup scallions, diced
- ½ teaspoon ground black pepper
- 1 teaspoon avocado oil

Directions:

1. Put the ground beef in the bowl and mix it up with flax meal, cilantro, garlic clove, chili pepper, egg, ground coriander, diced onion, and ground black pepper. When the mixture is homogenous, add shredded Cheddar cheese and stir the mixture with the help of the spoon.
2. Make the small meatballs from the ground beef mixture.
3. Then preheat the air fryer to 380F. Brush the air fryer basket with avocado oil from inside and arrange the prepared meatballs in one layer.
4. Cook them for 7 minutes or until the meatballs are light brown.

Garlic Pork And Bok Choy

Servings: 4
Cooking Time: 35 Minutes

Ingredients:

- 4 pork chops, boneless
- 1 bok choy head, torn
- 2 cups chicken stock
- 2 tablespoons coconut aminos
- 2 garlic cloves, minced
- A pinch of salt and black pepper
- 2 tablespoons coconut oil, melted

Directions:

1. Heat up a pan that fits the air fryer with the oil over medium-high heat, add the pork chops and brown for 5 minutes.
2. Add the garlic, salt and pepper and cook for another minute. Add the rest of the ingredients except the bok choy and cook at 380 degrees F for 25 minutes.
3. Add the bok choy, cook for 5 minutes more, divide everything between plates and serve.

Beef Sausage With Grilled Broccoli

Servings: 4
Cooking Time: 25 Minutes

Ingredients:

- 1 pound beef Vienna sausage
- 1/2 cup mayonnaise
- 1 teaspoon yellow mustard
- 1 tablespoon fresh lemon juice
- 1 teaspoon garlic powder
- 1/4 teaspoon black pepper
- 1 pound broccoli

Directions:

1. Start by preheating your Air Fryer to 380 degrees F. Spritz the grill pan with cooking oil.
2. Cut the sausages into serving sized pieces. Cook the sausages for 15 minutes, shaking the basket occasionally to get all sides browned. Set aside.
3. In the meantime, whisk the mayonnaise with mustard, lemon juice, garlic powder, and black pepper. Toss the broccoli with the mayo mixture.
4. Turn up temperature to 0 degrees F. Cook broccoli for 6 minutes, turning halfway through the cooking time.
5. Serve the sausage with the grilled broccoli on the side. Bon appétit!

Balsamic London Broil With Garlic

Servings: 8

Cooking Time: 30 Minutes + Marinating Time

Ingredients:

- 2 pounds London broil
- 3 large garlic cloves, minced
- 3 tablespoons balsamic vinegar
- 3 tablespoons whole-grain mustard
- 2 tablespoons olive oil
- Sea salt and ground black pepper, to taste
- 1/2 teaspoon dried hot red pepper flakes

Directions:

1. Score both sides of the cleaned London broil.
2. Thoroughly combine the remaining ingredients; massage this mixture into the meat to coat it on all sides. Let it marinate for at least 3 hours.
3. Set the Air Fryer to cook at 400 degrees F; Then cook the London broil for 15 minutes. Flip it over and cook another 10 to 12 minutes. Bon appétit!

Beef And Thyme Cabbage Mix

Servings: 4
Cooking Time: 25 Minutes

Ingredients:

- 2 pounds beef, cubed
- ½ pound bacon, chopped
- 2 shallots, chopped
- 1 napa cabbage, shredded
- 2 garlic cloves, minced
- A pinch of salt and black pepper
- 2 tablespoons olive oil
- 1 teaspoon thyme, dried
- 1 cup beef stock

Directions:

1. Heat up a pan that fits the air fryer with the oil over medium-high heat, add the beef and brown for 3 minutes.
2. Add the bacon, shallots and garlic and cook for 2 minutes more.
3. Add the rest of the ingredients, toss, put the pan in the air fryer and cook at 390 degrees F for 20 minutes. Divide between plates and serve.

Tri-Tip Skewers Hungarian Style

Servings: 3
Cooking Time: 12 Minutes

Ingredients:

- 1-lb beef tri-tip, sliced to 2-inch cubes
- 2 smashed garlic cloves
- a pinch of salt
- 2 teaspoons crushed caraway seeds
- 1 medium red onion, sliced into quarters
- 1 medium bell pepper seeded and cut into chunks
- 1/2 cup olive oil
- 1/2 teaspoon paprika

Directions:

1. In a shallow dish, mix well all Ingredients except for bell pepper and onion. Toss well to coat. Marinate in the ref for 3 hours.
2. Thread beef, onion, and bell pepper pieces in skewers. Place on skewer rack in air fryer.
3. For 12 minutes, cook on 0oF. Halfway through cooking time, turnover skewers. If needed, cook in batches.
4. Serve and enjoy.

Almond And Caraway Crust Steak

Servings: 4
Cooking Time: 16 Minutes

Ingredients:

- 1/3 cup almond flour
- 2 eggs
- 2 teaspoons caraway seeds
- 4 beef steaks
- 2 teaspoons garlic powder
- 1 tablespoon melted butter
- Fine sea salt and cayenne pepper, to taste

Directions:

1. Generously coat steaks with garlic powder, caraway seeds, salt, and cayenne pepper.
2. In a mixing dish, thoroughly combine melted butter with seasoned crumbs. In another bowl, beat the eggs until they're well whisked.
3. First, coat steaks with the beaten egg; then, coat beef steaks with the buttered crumb mixture.
4. Place the steaks in the Air Fryer cooking basket; cook for 10 minutes at 355 degrees F. Bon appétit!

Saucy Beef With Cotija Cheese

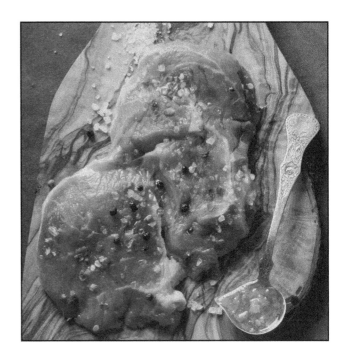

Servings: 3

Cooking Time: 27 Minutes

Ingredients:

- 2 ounces Cotija cheese, cut into sticks
- 2 teaspoons paprika
- 2 teaspoons dried thyme
- 1/2 cup shallots, peeled and chopped
- 3 beef tenderloins, cut in half lengthwise
- 2 teaspoons dried basil
- 1/3 cup homemade bone stock
- 2 tablespoon olive oil
- 3 cloves garlic, minced
- 1 ½ cups tomato puree, no sugar added
- 1 teaspoon ground black pepper, or more to taste
- 1 teaspoon fine sea salt, or more to taste

Directions:

1. Firstly, season the beef tenderloin with the salt, ground black pepper, and paprika; place a piece of the Cotija cheese in the middle.
2. Now, tie each tenderloin with a kitchen string; drizzle with olive oil and reserve.
3. Stir the garlic, shallots, bone stock, tomato puree into an oven safe bowl; cook in the preheated Air Fryer at 5 degrees F for 7 minutes.
4. Add the reserved beef along with basil and thyme. Set the timer for 1minutes. Eat warm and enjoy!

Rosemary Lamb Steak

Servings: 2
Cooking Time: 12 Minutes

Ingredients:

- 12 oz lamb steak (6 oz each lamb steak)
- 1 teaspoon dried rosemary
- 1 teaspoon minced onion
- 1 tablespoon avocado oil
- ½ teaspoon salt

Directions:

1. Rub the lamb steaks with minced onion and salt. In the shallow bowl mix up dried rosemary and avocado oil.
2. Sprinkle the meat with rosemary mixture.
3. After this, preheat the Air Fryer to 400F.
4. Put the lamb steaks in the Air Fryer in one layer and cook them for 6 minutes.
5. Then flip the meat on another side and cook it for 6 minutes more.

Coriander Lamb With Pesto 'n Mint Dip

Servings: 4
Cooking Time: 16 Minutes

Ingredients:

- 1 1/2 teaspoons coriander seeds, ground in spice mill or in mortar with pestle
- 1 large red bell pepper, cut into 1-inch squares
- 1 small red onion, cut into 1-inch squares
- 1 tablespoon extra-virgin olive oil plus additional for brushing
- 1 teaspoon coarse kosher salt
- 1-pound trimmed lamb meat, cut into 1 1/4-inch cubes
- 4 large garlic cloves, minced
- Mint-Pesto Dip Ingredients
- 1 cup (packed) fresh mint leaves
- 2 tablespoons pine nuts
- 2 tablespoons freshly grated Parmesan cheese
- 1 tablespoon fresh lemon juice
- 1 medium garlic clove, peeled
- 1/2 cup (packed) fresh cilantro leaves
- 1/2 teaspoon coarse kosher salt
- 1/2 cup (or more) extra-virgin olive oil

Directions:

1. In a blender, puree all dip Ingredients until smooth and creamy. Transfer to a bowl and set aside.
2. In a large bowl, mix well coriander, salt, garlic, and oil. Add lamb, toss well to coat. Marinate for at least an hour in the ref.
3. The thread lamb, bell pepper, and onion alternately in a skewer. Repeat until all Ingredients re used up. Place in skewer rack in Air Fryer.
4. For 8 minutes, cook on 390oF. Halfway through cooking time, turnover.
5. Serve and enjoy with sauce on the side.

Creamy Pork Schnitzel

Servings: 2
Cooking Time: 10 Minutes

Ingredients:

- 8 oz pork cutlets (4 oz each cutlet)
- 1 teaspoon sunflower oil
- 1 egg, beaten
- 1 tablespoon heavy cream
- ½ cup coconut flour
- ½ teaspoon ground black pepper
- ½ teaspoon salt

Directions:

1. Beat the pork cutlets with the help of the kitchen hammer and sprinkle them with ground black pepper and salt. After this, mix up egg and heavy cream.
2. Dip the pork cutlets in the egg mixture and then coat in the coconut flour. Repeat the same steps one more time.
3. Then preheat the air fryer to 400F. Sprinkle the pork cutlets with sunflower oil and put them in the Air Fryer.
4. Cook the schnitzels for 5 minutes from each side.

Beef And Plums Mix

Servings: 6
Cooking Time: 40 Minutes

Ingredients:

- 1½ pounds beef stew meat, cubed
- 3 tablespoons honey
- 2 tablespoons olive oil
- 9 ounces plums, pitted and halved
- 8 ounces beef stock
- 2 yellow onions, chopped
- 2 garlic cloves, minced
- Salt and black pepper to tastes
- 1 teaspoon turmeric powder
- 1 teaspoon ginger powder
- 1 teaspoon cinnamon powder

Directions:

1. In a pan that fits your air fryer, heat up the oil over medium heat.
2. Add the beef, stir, and brown for minutes.
3. Add the honey, onions, garlic, salt, pepper, turmeric, ginger, and cinnamon; toss, and cook for 2-minutes more.
4. Add the plums and the stock; toss again.
5. Place the pan in the fryer and cook at 380 degrees for 30 minutes.
6. Divide everything into bowls and serve.

Cardamom Lamb Mix

Servings: 2
Cooking Time: 20 Minutes

Ingredients:

- 10 oz lamb sirloin
- 1 oz fresh ginger, sliced
- 2 oz spring onions, chopped
- ¼ teaspoon ground cinnamon
- ½ teaspoon ground cardamom
- ½ teaspoon fennel seeds
- ½ teaspoon chili flakes
- ¼ teaspoon salt
- 1 tablespoon avocado oil

Directions:

1. Put the fresh ginger in the blender. Add onion, ground cardamom, cinnamon, fennel seeds, chili flakes, salt, and avocado oil. Blend the mixture until you get the smooth mass.
2. After this, make the small cuts in the lamb sirloin. Rub the meat with the blended spice mixture and leave it for 20 minutes to marinate.
3. Meanwhile, preheat the Air Fryer to 350F.
4. Put the marinated lamb sirloin in the Air Fryer and cook it for 20 minutes. Flip the meat on another side in halfway. Slice the cooked meat.

Egg Noodles, Ground Beef and Tomato Sauce Bake

Servings: 3
Cooking Time: 45 Minutes

Ingredients:

- 1 (15 ounce) can tomato sauce
- 4-ounce egg noodles, cooked according to manufacturer's directions
- 1/2-pound ground beef
- 1/2 teaspoon white sugar
- 1/2 teaspoon salt
- 1/2 teaspoon garlic salt
- 1/2 cup sour cream
- 1/2 large white onion, diced
- 1/4 cup shredded sharp Cheddar cheese, or more to taste
- 1.5-ounce cream cheese

Directions:

1. Lightly grease baking pan of air fryer with cooking spray. Add ground beef, for minutes cook on 360oF. Halfway through cooking time crumble beef.
2. When done cooking, discard excess fat.
3. Stir in tomato sauce, garlic salt, salt, and sugar. Mix well and cook for another 15 minutes. Transfer to a bowl.
4. In another bowl, whisk well onion, cream cheese, and sour cream.
5. Place half of the egg noodles on bottom of air fryer baking pan. Top with half of the sour cream mixture, then half the tomato sauce mixture. Repeat layering. And then top off with cheese.
6. Cover pan with foil.
7. Cook for another 15 minutes. Uncover and cook for another 5 minutes.
8. Serve and enjoy.

Easy Cheeseburger Meatballs

Servings: 3
Cooking Time: 15 Minutes

Ingredients:

- 1 pound ground pork
- 1 tablespoon coconut aminos
- 1 teaspoon garlic, minced
- 2 tablespoons spring onions, finely chopped
- 1/2 cup pork rinds
- 1/2 cup parmesan cheese, preferably freshly grated

Directions:

1. Combine the ground pork, coconut aminos, garlic, and spring onions in a mixing dish. Mix until everything is well incorporated.
2. Form the mixture into small meatballs.
3. In a shallow bowl, mix the pork rinds and grated parmesan cheese. Roll the meatballs over the parmesan mixture.
4. Cook at 380 degrees F for 3 minutes; shake the basket and cook an additional minutes or until meatballs are browned on all sides. Bon appétit!

Classic Smoked Pork Chops

Servings: 6
Cooking Time: 25 Minutes

Ingredients:

- 6 pork chops
- Hickory-smoked salt, to savor
- Ground black pepper, to savor
- 1 teaspoon onion powder
- 1/2 teaspoon garlic powder
- 1/2 teaspoon cayenne pepper
- 1/3 cup almond meal

Directions:

1. Simply place all of the above ingredients into a zip-top plastic bag; shake them up to coat well.
2. Spritz the chops with a pan spray (canola spray works well here) and transfer them to the Air Fryer cooking basket.
3. Roast them for 20 minutes at 5 degrees F. Serve with sautéed vegetables. Bon appétit!

Butter Beef

Servings: 4
Cooking Time: 10 Minutes

Ingredients:

- 4 beef steaks (3 oz each steak)
- 4 tablespoons butter, softened
- 1 teaspoon ground black pepper
- ½ teaspoon salt

Directions:

1. In the shallow bowl mix up softened butter, ground black pepper, and salt.
2. Then brush the beef steaks with the butter mixture from each side.
3. Preheat the Air Fryer to 400F.
4. Put the butter steaks in the Air Fryer and cook them for 5 minutes from each side.

Cumin Pork Steak

Servings: 4
Cooking Time: 25 Minutes

Ingredients:

- 16 oz pork steak (4 oz every steak)
- 1 tablespoon sesame oil
- ½ teaspoon ground paprika
- ½ teaspoon ground cumin
- ½ teaspoon salt
- ½ teaspoon dried garlic

Directions:

1. Sprinkle every pork steak with ground paprika, ground cumin, salt, and dried garlic. Then sprinkle the meat with sesame oil.
2. Preheat the Air Fryer to 400F.
3. Put the pork steak in the Air Fryer in one layer and cook them for minutes.
4. Then flip the steaks on another side and cook them for 10 minutes more.

Rib Eye Steak Recipe From Hawaii

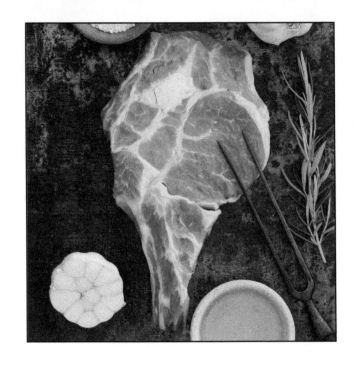

Servings: 6
Cooking Time: 45 Minutes

Ingredients:

- ½ cup soy sauce
- ½ cup sugar
- 1-inch ginger, grated
- 2 cups pineapple juice
- 2 teaspoons sesame oil
- 3 pounds rib eye steaks
- 5 tablespoon apple cider vinegar

Directions:

1. Combine all ingredients in a Ziploc bag and allow to marinate in the fridge for at least 2 hours.
2. Preheat the air fryer to 3900F.
3. Place the grill pan accessory in the air fryer.
4. Grill the meat for 15 minutes while flipping the meat every 8 minutes and cook in batches.
5. Meanwhile, pour the marinade in a saucepan and allow to simmer until the sauce thickens.
6. Brush the grilled meat with the glaze before serving.

Scallion Sauce On Lemongrass Chili Marinated Tri-Tip

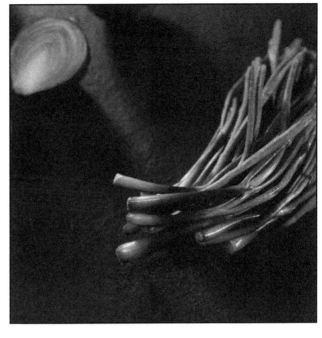

Servings: 4
Cooking Time: 20 Minutes

Ingredients:

- 1 cup canned unsweetened coconut milk
- 2 tablespoons packed light brown sugar
- 1 tablespoon fresh lime juice
- 6 garlic cloves
- 4 red or green Thai chiles, stemmed
- 2 lemongrass stalks, bottom third only, tough outer layers removed
- 1-pound tri-tip fat cap left on , cut into 1-inch cubes
- 1 1 1/2" piece ginger, peeled
- 1/4 cup fish sauce
- Scallion Dip Ingredients

- 15 scallions, very thinly sliced
- 3 tablespoons grapeseed oil
- 2 tablespoons black vinegar
- 2 tablespoons toasted sesame seeds
- 1/4 cup fish sauce

Basting Sauce Ingredients:

- 1 1/2 tablespoons fresh lime juice
- 1/2 cup canned unsweetened coconut milk
- 2 garlic cloves, crushed
- 3 tablespoons fish sauce

Directions:

1. Except for meat, puree all Ingredients in a blender. Transfer into a bowl and marinate beef at least overnight in the ref.
2. In a medium bowl, mix well all scallion dip Ingredients and set aside.
3. In a separate bowl mix all basting sauce Ingredients.
4. Thread meat into skewers and place on skewer rack in air fryer. Baste with sauce.
5. Cook for 10 minutes at 390 F or to desired doneness. Halfway through cooking time, baste and turnover skewers. Serve and enjoy with the dip on the side.

Beef Roast

Servings: 6
Cooking Time: 50 Minutes

Ingredients:

- 2½ pounds beef eye of round roast, trimmed
- 2 tablespoons olive oil
- ½ teaspoon onion powder
- ½ teaspoon garlic powder
- ½ teaspoon cayenne pepper
- ½ teaspoon ground black pepper
- Salt, to taste

Directions:

1. Preheat the Air fryer to 360 o F and grease an Air Fryer basket.
2. Rub the roast generously with all the spices and coat with olive oil.
3. Arrange the roast in the Air Fryer basket and cook for about 50 minutes.
4. Dish out the roast and cover with foil.
5. Cut into desired size slices and serve.

Keto Wiener Schnitzel

Servings: 2
Cooking Time: 20 Minutes

Ingredients:

- 1 egg, beaten
- 1/2 teaspoon ground black pepper
- 1 teaspoon paprika
- 1/2 teaspoon coarse sea salt
- 1 tablespoon ghee, melted
- 1/2 cup Romano cheese, grated
- 2 beef schnitzel

Directions:

1. Start by preheating your Air Fryer to 360 degrees F.
2. In a shallow bowl, whisk the egg with black pepper, paprika, and salt.
3. Thoroughly combine the ghee with the Romano cheese in another shallow bowl. Using a meat mallet, pound the schnitzel to 1/4-inch thick.
4. Dip the schnitzel into the egg mixture; then, roll the schnitzel over the Romano cheese mixture until coated on all sides.
5. Cook for 13 minutes in the preheated Air Fryer. Bon appétit!

Ribeye Steak With Classis Garlic Mayonnaise

Servings: 3
Cooking Time: 20 Minutes

Ingredients:

- 1 ½ pounds ribeye, bone-in
- 1 tablespoon butter, room temperature
- Salt, to taste
- 1/2 teaspoon crushed black pepper
- 1/2 teaspoon dried dill
- 1/2 teaspoon cayenne pepper
- 1/2 teaspoon garlic powder
- 1/2 teaspoon onion powder
- 1 teaspoon ground coriander
- 3 tablespoons mayonnaise
- 1 teaspoon garlic, minced

Directions:

1. Start by preheating your Air Fryer to 400 degrees F.
2. Pat dry the ribeye and rub it with softened butter on all sides. Sprinkle with seasonings and transfer to the cooking basket.
3. Cook in the preheated Air Fryer for 15 minutes, flipping them halfway through the cooking time.
4. In the meantime, simply mix the mayonnaise with garlic and place in the refrigerator until ready to serve. Bon appétit!

Simple Garlic 'n Herb Meatballs

Servings: 4

Cooking Time: 20 Minutes

Ingredients:

- 1 clove of garlic, minced
- 1 egg, beaten
- 1 tablespoon breadcrumbs or flour
- 1 teaspoon dried mixed herbs
- 1-pound lean ground beef

Directions:

1. Place all Ingredients in a mixing bowl and mix together using your hands.
2. Form small balls using your hands and set aside in the fridge to set.
3. Preheat the Air Fryer to 00F.
4. Place the meatballs in the Air Fryer basket and cook for 20 minutes.
5. Halfway through the cooking time, give the meatballs a shake to cook evenly.

Charred Onions 'n Steak Cube Bbq

Servings: 3
Cooking Time: 40 Minutes

Ingredients:

- 1 cup red onions, cut into wedges
- 1 tablespoon dry mustard
- 1 tablespoon olive oil
- 1-pound boneless beef sirloin, cut into cubes
- Salt and pepper to taste

Directions:

1. Preheat the Air Fryer to 3900F.
2. Place the grill pan accessory in the Air Fryer.
3. Toss all ingredients in a bowl and mix until everything is coated with the seasonings.
4. Place on the grill pan and cook for minutes.
5. Halfway through the cooking time, give a stir to cook evenly.

Bacon With Shallot And Greens

Servings: 2
Cooking Time: 10 Minutes

Ingredients:

- 7 ounces mixed greens
- 8 thick slices pork bacon
- 2 shallots, peeled and diced
- Nonstick cooking spray

Directions:

1. Begin by preheating the Air Fryer to 345 degrees F.
2. Now, add the shallot and bacon to the Air Fryer cooking basket; set the timer for minutes. Spritz with a nonstick cooking spray.
3. After that, pause the Air Fryer; throw in the mixed greens; give it a good stir and cook an additional 5 minutes. Serve warm.

Top Round Roast With Mustard Rosemary Thyme Blend

Servings: 10
Cooking Time: 1 Hour

Ingredients:

- 1 teaspoon dry mustard
- 2 teaspoons dried rosemary
- 3 tablespoons olive oil
- 4 pounds beef top round roast
- 4 teaspoons dried oregano
- 4 teaspoons dried thyme
- Salt and pepper to taste

Directions:

1. Preheat the Air Fryer for 5 minutes.
2. Place all ingredients in a baking dish that will fit in the Air Fryer.
3. Place the dish in the Air Fryer and cook for 1 hour at 50F.

Betty's Beef Roast

Servings: 2
Cooking Time: 25 Minutes

Ingredients:

- 2 lb. beef
- 1 tbsp. olive oil
- 1 tsp. dried rosemary
- 1 tsp. dried thyme
- ½ tsp. black pepper
- ½ tsp. oregano
- ½ tsp. garlic powder
- 1 tsp. salt
- 1 tsp. onion powder

Directions:

1. Preheat the Air Fryer to 330°F.
2. In a small bowl, mix together all of the spices.
3. Coat the beef with a brushing of olive oil.
4. Massage the spice mixture into the beef.
5. Transfer the meat to the Air Fryer and cook for 30 minutes. Turn it over and cook on the other side for another 2minutes

Garlic Chili Steak

Servings: 4
Cooking Time: 35 Minutes

Ingredients:

- 1-pound lamb sirloin
- 1 teaspoon chili paste
- 1 tablespoon avocado oil
- ½ teaspoon dried thyme
- ¼ teaspoon minced ginger
- ¼ teaspoon chili powder
- ½ teaspoon salt

Directions:

1. In the shallow bowl mix up chili paste, avocado oil, dried thyme, minced ginger, and chili powder.
2. Then sprinkle the lamb sirloin with salt and rub with chili paste mixture. Use the gloves for this step.
3. Leave the meat for at least minutes to marinate.
4. Preheat the Air Fryer to 355F.
5. Put the meat in the Air Fryer basket and cook it for 20 minutes.
6. Then flip the meat on another side and cook it for 15 minutes more.

Ginger, Garlic'n Pork Dumplings

Servings: 8
Cooking Time: 15 Minutes

Ingredients:

- ¼ teaspoon crushed red pepper
- ½ teaspoon sugar
- 1 tablespoon chopped fresh ginger
- 1 tablespoon chopped garlic
- 1 teaspoon canola oil
- 1 teaspoon toasted sesame oil
- 18 dumpling wrappers
- 2 tablespoons rice vinegar
- 2 teaspoons soy sauce
- 4 cups bok choy, chopped
- 4 ounces ground pork

Directions:

1. Heat oil in a skillet and sauté the ginger and garlic until fragrant. Stir in the ground pork and cook for 5 minutes.
2. Stir in the bok choy and crushed red pepper. Season with salt and pepper to taste. Allow to cool.
3. Place the meat mixture in the middle of the dumpling wrappers. Fold the wrappers to seal the meat mixture in.
4. Place the bok choy in the grill pan.
5. Cook the dumplings in the Air Fryer at 3300F for 1minutes.
6. Meanwhile, prepare the dipping sauce by combining the remaining Ingredients in a bowl.

Cinnamon Lamb Meatloaf

Servings: 4
Cooking Time: 35 Minutes

Ingredients:

- 2 pounds lamb, ground
- A pinch of salt and black pepper
- ½ teaspoon hot paprika
- A drizzle of olive oil
- 2 tablespoons parsley, chopped
- 2 tablespoons cilantro, chopped
- 1 teaspoon cumin, ground
- ¼ teaspoon cinnamon powder
- 1 teaspoon coriander, ground
- 1 egg
- 2 tablespoons keto tomato sauce
- 4 scallions, chopped
- 1 teaspoon lemon juice

Directions:

1. In a bowl, combine the lamb with the rest of the ingredients except the oil and stir really well.
2. Grease a loaf pan that fits the Air Fryer with the oil, add the lamb mix and shape the meatloaf.
3. Put the pan in the Air Fryer and cook at 380 degrees F for 35 minutes.
4. Slice and serve.

Pork Chops With Peanut Sauce

Servings: 4
Cooking Time: 12 Minutes

Ingredients:

For Chops:

- 1 teaspoon fresh ginger, minced
- 1 garlic clove, minced
- 2 tablespoons soy sauce
- 1 tablespoon olive oil
- 1 teaspoon hot pepper sauce
- 1-pound boneless pork chop, cubed into 1-inch size

For Peanut Sauce:

- 1 tablespoon olive oil
- 1 shallot, finely chopped
- 1 garlic clove, minced
- 1 teaspoon ground coriander
- ¾ cup ground peanuts
- 1 teaspoon hot pepper sauce
- ¾ cup coconut milk

Directions:

1. For pork: in a bowl, mix together the ginger, garlic, soy sauce, oil, and hot pepper sauce.
2. Add the pork chops and generously coat with mixture.
3. Place at the room temperature for about 15 minutes.
4. Set the temperature of air fryer to 390 degrees F. Grease an Air Fryer basket.
5. Arrange chops into the prepared air fryer basket in a single layer.
6. Air fry for about 12 minutes.
7. Meanwhile, for the sauce: in a pan, heat oil over medium heat and sauté the shallot and garlic for about 2-3 minutes.
8. Add the coriander and sauté for about 1 minute.
9. Stir in the remaining ingredients and cook for about 5 minutes, stirring continuously.
10. Remove the pan of sauce from heat and let it cool slightly.
11. Remove the chops from air fryer and transfer onto serving plates.
12. Serve immediately with the topping of peanut sauce.

Italian Beef Roast

Servings: 10
Cooking Time: 3 Hours

Ingredients:

- ¼ teaspoon black pepper
- ½ cup water
- ½ teaspoon thyme
- 1 onion, sliced thinly
- 1 teaspoon basil
- 1 teaspoon salt
- 2 ½ pounds beef round roast
- 4 tablespoons olive oil

Directions:

1. Place all ingredients in a baking dish and make sure that the entire surface of the beef is coated with the spices.
2. Place the baking dish with the bee in the Air Fryer. Close.
3. Cook for hours at 4000F.

Perfect Thai Meatballs

Servings: 4
Cooking Time: 20 Minutes

Ingredients:

- 1 pound ground beef
- 1 teaspoon red Thai curry paste
- 1/2 lime, rind and juice
- 1 teaspoon Chinese spice
- 2 teaspoons lemongrass, finely chopped
- 1 tablespoon sesame oil

Directions:

1. Thoroughly combine all ingredients in a mixing dish.
2. Shape into meatballs and place them into the Air Fryer cooking basket. Cook at 380 degrees F for 10 minutes; pause the machine and cook for a further 5 minutes, or until cooked through.
3. Serve accompanied by the dipping sauce. Bon appétit!

Italian Beef Meatballs

Servings: 6
Cooking Time: 15 Minutes

Ingredients:

- 2 large eggs
- 2 pounds ground beef
- ¼ cup fresh parsley, chopped
- 1¼ cups panko breadcrumbs
- ¼ cup Parmigiano Reggiano, grated
- 1 teaspoon dried oregano
- 1 small garlic clove, chopped
- Salt and black pepper, to taste
- 1 teaspoon vegetable oil

Directions:

1. Preheat the Air Fryer to 350 o F and grease an Air Fryer basket.
2. Mix beef with all other ingredients in a bowl until well combined.
3. Make equal-sized balls from the mixture and arrange the balls in the Air Fryer basket.
4. Cook for about 13 minutes and dish out to serve warm.

Pesto Coated Rack Of Lamb

Servings: 4
Cooking Time: 15 Minutes

Ingredients:

- ½ bunch fresh mint
- 1 (1½-pounds) rack of lamb
- 1 garlic clove
- ¼ cup extra-virgin olive oil
- ½ tablespoon honey
- Salt and black pepper, to taste

Directions:

1. Preheat the Air Fryer to 200 o F and grease an Air Fryer basket.
2. Put the mint, garlic, oil, honey, salt, and black pepper in a blender and pulse until smooth to make pesto.
3. Coat the rack of lamb with this pesto on both sides and arrange in the Air Fryer basket.
4. Cook for about 15 minutes and cut the rack into individual chops to serve.

Spicy Holiday Roast Beef

Servings: 8
Cooking Time: 50 Minutes

Ingredients:

- 2 pounds roast beef, at room temperature
- 2 tablespoons extra-virgin olive oil
- 1 teaspoon sea salt flakes
- 1 teaspoon black pepper, preferably freshly ground
- 1 teaspoon smoked paprika
- A few dashes of liquid smoke
- 2 jalapeño peppers, thinly sliced

Directions:

1. Start by preheating the Air Fryer to 330 degrees F.
2. Then, pat the roast dry using kitchen towels. Rub with extra-virgin olive oil and all seasonings along with liquid smoke.
3. Roast for minutes in the preheated Air Fryer; then, pause the machine and turn the roast over; roast for additional 15 minutes.
4. Check for doneness using a meat thermometer and serve sprinkled with sliced jalapeños. Bon appétit!

Mediterranean Crescent Squares

Servings: 6
Cooking Time: 20 Minutes

Ingredients:

- 6 slices Asiago cheese
- 1/2 teaspoon oregano
- 1/3 teaspoon fresh or dried rosemary, chopped
- 6 slices prosciutto
- 1 teaspoon salt
- 1/2 teaspoon basil
- 1 teaspoon freshly ground black pepper
- 1/3teaspoon smoked paprika
- ½ can crescent roll, refrigerated
- 1/3 teaspoon fresh or dried thyme, chopped
- 1/2 tablespoon fresh coriander, minced
- 6 well-beaten eggs

Directions:

1. Unroll the crescent rolls and form six rectangles. Gently fold up the edges of each rectangle and transfer them to the Air Fryer basket.
2. Now, crack 1 egg into each rectangle. Sprinkle with the rosemary, thyme, basil, oregano, salt, ground black pepper, paprika, and minced coriander.
3. Add 1 piece of prosciutto and top with 1 slice of Asiago cheese. Repeat with the remaining rectangles.
4. Bake for 12 minutes at 292 degrees F and serve warm.

Fast Lamb Ribs

Servings: 4
Cooking Time: 14 Minutes

Ingredients:

- 4 lamb ribs
- 4 garlic cloves, minced
- 1 cup veggie stock
- ½ teaspoon chili powder
- ¼ teaspoon smoked paprika
- 2 tablespoons extra virgin olive oil
- Salt and black pepper to taste

Directions:

1. In a bowl, combine all of the ingredients—except the ribs—and mix well.
2. Then add the ribs and rub them thoroughly with the mixture.
3. Transfer the ribs to your Air Fryer's basket and cook at 0 degrees F for 7 minutes on each side.
4. Serve with a side salad.

French-Style Pork And Pepper Meatloaf

Servings: 4
Cooking Time: 35 Minutes

Ingredients:

- 1 pound pork, ground
- 1/2 cup parmesan cheese, grated
- 1 ½ tablespoons green garlic, minced
- 1½ tablespoon fresh cilantro, minced
- 1/2 tablespoon fish sauce
- 1/3 teaspoon dried basil
- 1 leek, chopped
- 1 serrano pepper, chopped
- 2 tablespoons tomato puree
- 1/2 teaspoons dried thyme
- Salt and ground black pepper, to taste

Directions:

1. Add all ingredients to a large-sized mixing dish and combine everything using your hands.
2. Then, form a meatloaf using a spatula.
3. Bake for 2minutes at 365 degrees F. Afterward, allow your meatloaf to rest for 10 minutes before slicing and serving. Bon appétit!

Beef Quesadillas

Servings: 4
Cooking Time: 25 Minutes

Ingredients:

- 1 pound beefsteak, sliced
- 1 cup mozzarella cheese, grated
- ½ cup fresh cilantro, chopped
- 1 jalapeno chili, chopped
- 1 cup corn kernels, canned
- Salt and black pepper
- Oil for greasing

Directions:

1. Place sliced beef on each taco, top with cheese, cilantro, chili, corn, salt and pepper. Fold in half and secure with toothpicks.
2. Grease the rack with oil and arrange the tacos into the basket.
3. Cook at 380 F for minutes, turning once halfway through. Serve with guacamole.

Mint And Rosemary Lamb

Servings: 2
Cooking Time: 35 Minutes

Ingredients:

- 12 oz leg of lamb, boneless
- 1 teaspoon dried rosemary
- ½ teaspoon dried mint
- 1 garlic clove, diced
- ½ teaspoon salt
- ¼ teaspoon ground black pepper
- 1 teaspoon apple cider vinegar
- 1 tablespoon olive oil

Directions:

1. In the mixing bowl mix up dried rosemary, mint, diced garlic, salt, ground black pepper, apple cider vinegar, and olive oil.
2. Then rub the leg of lamb with the spice mixture and leave for 2 hours to marinate.
3. After this, preheat the air fryer to 400F. Put the leg of lamb in the Air Fryer and sprinkle with all remaining spice mixture.
4. Cook the meal for 25 minutes.
5. Then flip the meat on another side and cook it for minutes more.

Parmesan Lamb Cutlets

Servings: 4
Cooking Time: 30 Minutes

Ingredients:

- 8 lamb cutlets
- A pinch of salt and black pepper
- 3 tablespoons mustard
- 3 tablespoons olive oil
- ½ cup coconut flakes
- ¼ cup parmesan, grated
- 2 tablespoons parsley, chopped
- 2 tablespoons chives, chopped
- 1 tablespoon rosemary, chopped

Directions:

1. In a bowl, mix the lamb cutlets with all the ingredients except the parmesan and the coconut flakes and toss well.
2. Dredge the cutlets in parmesan and coconut flakes, put them in your Air Fryer's basket and cook at 390 degrees F for minutes on each side.
3. Divide between plates and serve.

Herbed Leg Of Lamb

Servings: 5
Cooking Time: 75 Minutes

Ingredients:

- 2 pounds bone-in leg of lamb
- 2 tablespoons olive oil
- Salt and ground black pepper, as required
- 2 fresh rosemary sprigs
- 2 fresh thyme sprigs

Directions:

1. Coat the leg of lamb with oil and sprinkle with salt and black pepper.
2. Wrap the leg of lamb with herb sprigs.
3. Set the temperature of Air Fryer to 0 degrees F. Grease an Air Fryer basket.
4. Place leg of lamb into the prepared Air Fryer basket.
5. Air fry for about 7 minutes.
6. Remove from Air Fryer and transfer the leg of lamb onto a platter.
7. With a piece of foil, cover the leg of lamb for about 10 minutes before slicing.
8. Cut the leg of lamb into desired size pieces and serve.

Balsamic Pork Chops

Servings: 4
Cooking Time: 25 Minutes

Ingredients:

- 4 pork chops
- 1 tablespoon smoked paprika
- 1 tablespoon olive oil
- 2 tablespoons balsamic vinegar
- ½ cup chicken stock
- A pinch of salt and black pepper

Directions:

1. In a bowl, mix the pork chops with the rest of the ingredients and toss.
2. Put the pork chops in your Air Fryer's basket and cook at 390 degrees F for 25 minutes.
3. Divide between plates and serve.

Garlic Butter Pork Chops

Servings: 4
Cooking Time: 8 Minutes

Ingredients:

- 4 pork chops
- 1 tablespoon coconut butter
- 2 teaspoons parsley
- 1 tablespoon coconut oil
- 2 teaspoons garlic, grated
- Salt and black pepper, to taste

Directions:

1. Preheat the Air Fryer to 350 o F and grease an Air Fryer basket.
2. Mix all the seasonings, coconut oil, garlic, butter, and parsley in a bowl and coat the pork chops with it.
3. Cover the chops with foil and refrigerate to marinate for about 1 hour.
4. Remove the foil and arrange the chops in the Air Fryer basket.
5. Cook for about 8 minutes and dish out in a bowl to serve warm.

Smoked Beef Roast

Servings: 8
Cooking Time: 45 Minutes

Ingredients:

- 2 lb. roast beef, at room temperature
- 2 tbsp. extra-virgin olive oil
- 1 tsp. sea salt flakes
- 1 tsp. black pepper, preferably freshly ground
- 1 tsp. smoked paprika
- Few dashes of liquid smoke
- 2 jalapeño peppers, thinly sliced

Directions:

1. Pre-heat the Air Fryer to 330°F.
2. With kitchen towels, pat the beef dry.
3. Massage the extra-virgin olive oil and seasonings into the meat. Cover with liquid smoke.
4. Place the beef in the Air Fryer and roast for 30 minutes. Flip the roast over and allow to cook for another 15 minutes.
5. When cooked through, serve topped with sliced jalapeños.

Favorite Beef Stroganoff

Servings: 4

Cooking Time: 20 Minutes + Marinating Time

Ingredients:

- 1 ¼ pounds beef sirloin steak, cut into small-sized strips
- 1/4 cup balsamic vinegar
- 1 tablespoon brown mustard
- 1 tablespoon butter
- 1 cup beef broth
- 1 cup leek, chopped
- 2 cloves garlic, crushed
- 1 teaspoon cayenne pepper
- Sea salt flakes and crushed red pepper, to taste
- 1 cup sour cream
- 2 ½ tablespoons tomato paste

Directions:

1. Place the beef along with the balsamic vinegar and the mustard in a mixing dish; cover and marinate in your refrigerator for about hour.
2. Butter the inside of a baking dish and put the beef into the dish.
3. Add the broth, leeks and garlic. Cook at 0 degrees for 8 minutes. Pause the machine and add the cayenne pepper, salt, red pepper, sour cream and tomato paste; cook for additional 7 minutes.
4. Bon appétit!

Fish and Sea Food

Salmon And Garlic Sauce

Servings: 2
Cooking Time: 15 Minutes

Ingredients:

- 3 tablespoons parsley, chopped 4 salmon fillets, boneless
- ¼ cup ghee, melted
- 2 garlic cloves, minced 4 shallots, chopped
- Salt and black pepper to the taste

Directions:

1. Heat up a pan that fits the Air Fryer with the ghee over medium- high heat, add the garlic, shallots, salt, pepper and the parsley, stir and cook for 5 minutes.
2. Add the salmon fillets, toss gently, introduce the pan in the Air Fryer and cook at 380 degrees F for minutes.
3. Divide between plates and serve.

Crispy Mustardy Fish Fingers

Servings: 4
Cooking Time: 20 Minutes

Ingredients:

- 1 ½ pounds tilapia pieces (fingers)
- 1/2 cup all-purpose flour
- 2 eggs
- 1 tablespoon yellow mustard 1 cup cornmeal
- 1 teaspoon garlic powder 1 teaspoon onion powder
- Sea salt and ground black pepper, to taste 1/2 teaspoon celery powder
- 2 tablespoons peanut oil

Directions:

1. Pat dry the fish fingers with a kitchen towel.
2. To make a breading station, place the all-purpose flour in a shallow dish. In a separate dish, whisk the eggs with mustard.
3. In a third bowl, mix the remaining ingredients.
4. Dredge the fish fingers in the flour, shaking the excess into the bowl; dip in the egg mixture and turn to coat evenly; then, dredge in the cornmeal mixture, turning a couple of times to coat evenly.
5. Cook in the preheated Air Fryer at 390 degrees F for minutes; turn them over and cook another 5 minutes. Enjoy!

Cod And Cauliflower Patties

Servings: 4
Cooking Time: 12 Minutes

Ingredients:

- ½ cup cauliflower, shredded 4 oz cod fillet, chopped
- 1 egg, beaten
- 1 teaspoon chives, chopped
- ¼ teaspoon chili flakes
- 1 teaspoon salt
- ½ teaspoon ground cumin
- 2 tablespoons coconut flour
- 1 spring onion, chopped
- 1 tablespoon sesame oil

Directions:

1. Grind the chopped cod fillet and put it in the mixing bowl.
2. Add shredded cauliflower, egg, chives, chili flakes, salt, ground cumin, and chopped onion.
3. Stir the mixture until homogenous and add coconut flour. Stir it again.
4. After this, make the medium size patties.
5. Preheat the Air Fryer to 385F.
6. Place the patties in the Air Fryer basket and sprinkle with sesame oil. Cook the fish patties for 8 minutes.
7. Then flip them on another side and cook for 4 minutes more or until the patties are light brown.

Cajun Cod Fillets With Avocado Sauce

Servings: 2
Cooking Time: 20 Minutes

Ingredients:

- 2 cod fish fillets
- 1 egg
- Sea salt, to taste
- 1/2 cup tortilla chips, crushed
- 2 teaspoons olive oil
- 1/2 avocado, peeled, pitted, and mashed
- 1 tablespoon mayonnaise
- 3 tablespoons sour cream

- 1/2 teaspoon yellow mustard
- 1 teaspoon lemon juice
- 1 garlic clove, minced
- 1/4 teaspoon black pepper
- 1/4 teaspoon salt
- 1/4 teaspoon hot pepper sauce

Directions:

1. Start by preheating your Air Fryer to 360 degrees F. Spritz the Air Fryer basket with cooking oil.
2. Pat dry the fish fillets with a kitchen towel. Beat the egg in a shallow bowl.
3. In a separate bowl, thoroughly combine the salt, crushed tortilla chips, and olive oil.
4. Dip the fish into the egg, then, into the crumb mixture, making sure to coat thoroughly
5. Cook in the preheated Air Fryer approximately 12 minutes.
6. Meanwhile, make the avocado sauce by mixing the remaining ingredients in a bowl. Place in your refrigerator until ready to serve.
7. Serve the fish fillets with chilled avocado sauce on the side. Bon appétit!

Grilled Scallops With Pesto

Servings: 3
Cooking Time: 15 Minutes

Ingredients:

- ½ cup prepared commercial pesto
- 12 large scallops, side muscles removed
- Salt and pepper to taste

Directions:

1. Place all ingredients in a Ziploc bag and allow the scallops to marinate in the fridge for at least 2 hours.
2. Preheat the Air Fryer to 3900F.
3. Place the grill pan accessory in the Air Fryer.
4. Grill the scallops for 15 minutes.
5. Serve on pasta or bread if desired.

Snapper Fillets With Thai Sauce

Servings: 2
Cooking Time: 30 Minutes + Marinating Time

Ingredients:

- 1/2 cup full-fat coconut milk
- 2 tablespoons lemon juice
- 1 teaspoon fresh ginger, grated
- 2 snapper fillets
- 1 tablespoon olive oil
- Salt and white pepper, to taste

Directions:

1. Place the milk, lemon juice, and ginger in a glass bowl; add fish and let it marinate for hour.
2. Removed the fish from the milk mixture and place in the Air Fryer basket. Drizzle olive oil all over the fish fillets.
3. Cook in the preheated Air Fryer at 0 degrees F for 15 minutes.
4. Meanwhile, heat the milk mixture over medium-high heat; bring to a rapid boil, stirring continuously. Reduce to simmer and add the salt, and pepper; continue to cook 12 minutes more.
5. Spoon the sauce over the warm snapper fillets and serve immediately. Bon appétit!

Lemon Crab Patties

Servings: 4
Cooking Time: 10 Minutes

Ingredients:

- 1 egg
- 12 oz crabmeat
- 2 green onion, chopped
- 1/4 cup mayonnaise
- 1 cup almond flour
- 1 tsp old bay seasoning
- 1 tsp red pepper flakes
- 1 tbsp fresh lemon juice

Directions:

1. Preheat the Air Fryer to 400 F.
2. Spray air fryer basket with cooking spray.
3. Add 1/2 almond flour into the mixing bowl.
4. Add remaining ingredients and mix until well combined.
5. Make patties from mixture and coat with remaining almond flour and place into the Air Fryer basket.
6. Cook patties for 5 minutes then turn to another side and cook for 5 minutes more.
7. Serve and enjoy.

Char And Fennel

Servings: 4
Cooking Time: 18 Minutes

Ingredients:

- 4 char fillets, boneless
- 3 tablespoons olive oil
- 1 fennel bulb, sliced with a mandolin
- A pinch of salt and black pepper
- 5 garlic cloves, minced
- 1 teaspoon caraway seeds
- 2 tablespoons balsamic vinegar
- 1 tablespoon lemon juice
- 1 tablespoon lemon peel, grated
- ½ cup dill, chopped

Directions:

1. In a pan that fits your Air Fryer, mix the fish with all the other ingredients, toss, introduce in the Air Fryer and cook at 390 degrees F for minutes.
2. Divide the fish between plates and serve with a side salad.

Crab Legs

Servings: 3
Cooking Time: 20 Minutes

Ingredients:

- 3 lb. crab legs
- ¼ cup salted butter, melted and divided
- ½ lemon, juiced
- ¼ tsp. garlic powder

Directions:

1. In a bowl, toss the crab legs and two tablespoons of the melted butter together. Place the crab legs in the basket of the Fryer.
2. Cook at 400°F for fifteen minutes, giving the basket a good shake halfway through.
3. Combine the remaining butter with the lemon juice and garlic powder.
4. Crack open the cooked crab legs and remove the meat.
5. Serve with the butter dip on the side and enjoy!

Shrimp With Veggie

Servings: 4
Cooking Time: 20 Minutes

Ingredients:

- 50 small shrimp
- 1 tbsp Cajun seasoning
- 1 bag of frozen mix vegetables
- 1 tbsp olive oil

Directions:

1. Line Air Fryer basket with aluminum foil.
2. Add all ingredients into the large mixing bowl and toss well.
3. Transfer shrimp and vegetable mixture into the Air Fryer basket and cook at 0 F for 10 minutes.
4. Toss well and cook for 10 minutes more.
5. Serve and enjoy.

Salmon Mixed Eggs

Servings: 2
Cooking Time: 25 Minutes

Ingredients:

- 1 lb. salmon, cooked
- 2 eggs
- 1 onion, chopped
- 1 cup celery, chopped
- 1 tbsp. oil
- Salt and pepper to taste

Directions:

1. In a bowl, mix the eggs with a whisk. Stir in the celery, onion, salt and pepper.
2. Grease a round baking tray with the oil.
3. Transfer the egg mixture to the tray.
4. Cook in the Air Fryer on 300°F for 10 minutes.
5. Serve with cooked salmon.

Delicious Seafood Pie

Servings: 3
Cooking Time: 1 Hour

Ingredients:

- 1 lb russet potatoes, peeled and quartered
- 1 cup water
- 1 carrot, grated
- ½ head baby fennel, grated
- 1 bunch dill sprigs, chopped
- 1 sprig parsley, chopped
- A handful of baby spinach
- 1 small tomato, diced
- ½ celery sticks, grated
- 2 tbsp butter
- 1 tbsp milk
- ½ cup grated Cheddar cheese
- 1 small red chili, minced
- ½ lemon, juiced
- Salt and pepper to taste

Directions:

1. Add the potatoes to a pan, pour the water, and bring to a boil over medium heat on a stovetop. Use a fork to check that if they are soft and mash-able, after about minutes. Drain the water and use a potato masher to mash.
2. Add the butter, milk, salt, and pepper. Mash until smooth; set aside.
3. In a bowl, add the celery, carrots, cheese, chili, fennel, parsley, lemon juice, seafood mix, dill, tomato, spinach, salt, and pepper; mix well.
4. Preheat Air Fryer to 0 F. In a casserole dish, add half of the carrot mixture. Top with half of the potato mixture and level.
5. Place the dish in the air fryer and bake for 20 minutes until golden brown and the seafood is properly cooked. Remove the dish and add the remaining seafood mixture and level out.
6. Top with the remaining potato mash and level it too.
7. Place the dish back to the fryer and cook at 330 F for 20 minutes.
8. Once ready, ensure that it's well cooked, and remove the dish. Slice the pie and serve.

Lemony And Spicy Coconut Crusted Salmon

Servings: 4
Cooking Time: 6 Minutes

Ingredients:

* 1 pound salmon
* ½ cup flour
* 2 egg whites
* ½ cup breadcrumbs
* ½ cup unsweetened coconut, shredded
* ¼ teaspoon lemon zest
* Salt and freshly ground black pepper, to taste
* ¼ teaspoon cayenne pepper
* ¼ teaspoon red pepper flakes, crushed
* Vegetable oil, as required

Directions:

1. Preheat the Air Fryer to 400 o F and grease an Air Fryer basket.
2. Mix the flour, salt and black pepper in a shallow dish.
3. Whisk the egg whites in a second shallow dish.
4. Mix the breadcrumbs, coconut, lime zest, salt and cayenne pepper in a third shallow dish.
5. Coat salmon in the flour, then dip in the egg whites and then into the breadcrumb mixture evenly.
6. Place the salmon in the Air Fryer basket and drizzle with vegetable oil.
7. Cook for about 6 minutes and dish out to serve warm.

Garlic Parmesan Shrimp

Servings: 2
Cooking Time: 10 Minutes

Ingredients:

- 1 pound shrimp, deveined and peeled
- ½ cup parmesan cheese, grated
- ¼ cup cilantro, diced
- 1 tablespoon olive oil
- 1 teaspoon salt
- 1 teaspoon fresh cracked pepper
- 1 tablespoon lemon juice
- 6 garlic cloves, diced

Directions:

1. Preheat the Air Fryer to 350 o F and grease an Air Fryer basket.
2. Drizzle shrimp with olive oil and lemon juice and season with garlic, salt and cracked pepper.
3. Cover the bowl with plastic wrap and refrigerate for about hours.
4. Stir in the parmesan cheese and cilantro to the bowl and transfer to the Air Fryer basket.
5. Cook for about 10 minutes and serve immediately.

Appetizing Tuna Patties

Servings: 6
Cooking Time: 10 Minutes

Ingredients:

* 2 (6-ounce) cans tuna, drained
* ½ cup panko bread crumbs
* 1 egg
* 2 tablespoons fresh parsley, chopped
* 2 teaspoons Dijon mustard
* Dash of Tabasco sauce
* Salt and black pepper, to taste
* 1 tablespoon fresh lemon juice
* 1 tablespoon olive oil

Directions:

1. Preheat the Air Fryer to 355 o F and line a baking tray with foil paper.
2. Mix all the ingredients in a large bowl until well combined.
3. Make equal sized patties from the mixture and refrigerate overnight.
4. Arrange the patties on the baking tray and transfer to an Air Fryer basket.
5. Cook for about 10 minutes and dish out to serve warm.

Smoked Fish Quiche

Servings: 5
Cooking Time: 35 Minutes

Ingredients:

- 5 eggs, lightly beaten
- 4 tbsp heavy cream
- ¼ cup finely chopped green onions
- ¼ cup chopped parsley
- 1 tsp baking powder
- Salt and black pepper
- 1 lb smoked fish
- 1 cup shredded mozzarella cheese

Directions:

1. In a bowl, whisk eggs, cream, scallions, parsley, baking powder, salt and black.
2. Add in fish and cheese, stir to combine.
3. Line the Air Fryer with baking paper.
4. Pour the mixture into the pastry case and place it gently inside the Air Fryer.
5. Cook for 25 minutes at 360 F.
6. Check past minutes, so it's not overcooked.

Lemon Branzino

Servings: 4
Cooking Time: 8 Minutes

Ingredients:

- 1-pound branzino, trimmed, washed
- 1 teaspoon Cajun seasoning
- 1 tablespoon sesame oil
- 1 tablespoon lemon juice
- 1 teaspoon salt

Directions:

1. Rub the branzino with salt and Cajun seasoning carefully.
2. Then sprinkle the fish with the lemon juice and sesame oil.
3. Preheat the Air Fryer to 380F.
4. Place the fish in the Air Fryer and cook it for 8 minutes.

Soy-Orange Flavored Squid

Servings: 4
Cooking Time: 10 Minutes

Ingredients:

- ½ cup mirin
- 1 cup soy sauce
- 1/3 cup yuzu or orange juice, freshly squeezed
- 2 cups water
- 2 pounds squid body, cut into rings

Directions:

1. Place all ingredients in a Ziploc bag and allow the squid rings to marinate in the fridge for at least 2 hours.
2. Preheat the Air Fryer to 3900F.
3. Place the grill pan accessory in the Air Fryer.
4. Grill the squid rings for 10 minutes.
5. Meanwhile, pour the marinade over a sauce pan and allow to simmer for 10 minutes or until the sauce has reduced.
6. Baste the squid rings with the sauce before serving.

Japanese Ponzu Marinated Tuna

Servings: 4
Cooking Time: 10 Minutes + Marinate Time

Ingredients:

- 1 cup Japanese ponzu sauce
- 2 tbsp sesame oil
- 1 tbsp red pepper flakes
- 2 tbsp ginger paste
- ¼ cup scallions, sliced
- Salt and black pepper to taste

Directions:

1. In a bowl, mix the ponzu sauce, sesame oil, red pepper flakes, ginger paste, salt, and black pepper. Add in the tuna and toss to coat.
2. Cover and leave to marinate for 60 minutes in the fridge.
3. Preheat Air Fryer to 380 F. Spray Air Fryer basket with cooking spray.
4. Remove tuna from the fridge and arrange on the Air Fryer basket.
5. Cook for 6 minutes, turning once.
6. Top with scallions to serve.

Honey-Ginger Soy Sauce Over Grilled Tuna

Servings: 3
Cooking Time: 20 Minutes

Ingredients:

- 1 ½ pounds tuna, thick slices
- 1 serrano chili, seeded and minced
- 2 tablespoons grated fresh ginger
- 2 tablespoons honey
- 2 tablespoons peanut oil
- 2 tablespoons rice vinegar
- 2 tablespoons soy sauce

Directions:

1. Place all ingredients in a Ziploc bag.
2. Allow to marinate in the fridge for at least hours.
3. Preheat the Air Fryer to 00F.
4. Place the grill pan accessory in the Air Fryer.
5. Grill the fish for 1to 20 minutes.
6. Flip the fish halfway through the cooking time.
7. Meanwhile, pour the marinade in a saucepan and allow to simmer for 10 minutes until the sauce thickens.
8. Brush the tuna with the sauce before serving.

Coconut Shrimp

Servings: 4
Cooking Time: 12 Minutes

Ingredients:

- 1 tablespoon ghee, melted
- 1 pound shrimp, peeled and deveined
- ¼ cup coconut cream
- A pinch of red pepper flakes
- A pinch of salt and black pepper
- 1 tablespoon parsley, chopped
- 1 tablespoon chives, chopped

Directions:

1. In a pan that fits the fryer, combine all the ingredients except the parsley, put the pan in the Fryer and cook at 360 degrees F for minutes.
2. Divide the mix into bowls, sprinkle the parsley on top and serve.

Catfish With Spring Onions And Avocado

Servings: 4
Cooking Time: 15 Minutes

Ingredients:

- 2 teaspoons oregano, dried
- 2 teaspoons cumin, ground
- 2 teaspoons sweet paprika
- A pinch of salt and black pepper
- 4 catfish fillets
- 1 avocado, peeled and cubed
- ½ cup spring onions, chopped
- 2 tablespoons cilantro, chopped
- 2 teaspoons olive oil
- 2 tablespoons lemon juice

Directions:

1. In a bowl, mix all the ingredients except the fish and toss.
2. Arrange this in a baking pan that fits the Air Fryer, top with the fish, introduce the pan in the machine and cook at 360 degrees F for minutes, flipping the fish halfway.
3. Divide between plates and serve.

Easy Bacon Shrimp

Servings: 4
Cooking Time: 7 Minutes

Ingredients:

- 16 shrimp, deveined
- 1/4 tsp pepper
- 16 bacon slices

Directions:

1. Preheat the Air Fryer to 390 F.
2. Spray Air Fryer basket with cooking spray.
3. Wrap shrimp with bacon slice and place into the Air Fryer basket and cook for 5 minutes.
4. Turn shrimp to another side and cook for 2 minutes more. Season shrimp with pepper.
5. Serve and enjoy.

Tuna Stuffed Avocado

Servings: 2
Cooking Time: 12 Minutes

Ingredients:

- 1 avocado, pitted, halved
- ½ pound smoked tuna, boneless and shredded
- 1 egg, beaten
- ½ teaspoon salt
- ½ teaspoon chili powder
- ½ teaspoon ground nutmeg
- 1 teaspoon dried parsley
- Cooking spray

Directions:

1. Scoop ½ part of the avocado meat from the avocado to get the avocado boats. Use the scooper for this step.
2. After this, in the mixing bowl mix up tuna and egg. Shred the mixture with the help of the fork. Add salt, chili powder, ground nutmeg, and dried parsley. Stir the tuna mixture until homogenous.
3. Add the scooped avocado meat and mix up the mixture well.
4. Fill the avocado boats with tuna mixture.
5. Preheat the Air Fryer to 385F.
6. Arrange the tuna boats in the Air Fryer basket and cook them for minutes.

Salmon Patties

Servings: 4
Cooking Time: 20 Minutes

Ingredients:

- 1 egg
- 14 oz. canned salmon, drained
- 4 tbsp. flour
- 4 tbsp. cup cornmeal
- 4 tbsp. onion, minced
- ½ tsp. garlic powder
- 2 tbsp. mayonnaise
- Salt and pepper to taste

Directions:

1. Flake apart the salmon with a fork.
2. Put the flakes in a bowl and combine with the garlic powder, mayonnaise, flour, cornmeal, egg, onion, pepper, and salt.
3. Use your hands to shape equal portions of the mixture into small patties and put each one in the Air Fryer basket.
4. Air fry the salmon patties at 350°F for 15 minutes.
5. Serve hot.

Spicy Shrimp

Servings: 2
Cooking Time: 6 Minutes

Ingredients:

- 1/2 lb shrimp, peeled and deveined
- 1/2 tsp old bay seasoning
- 1 tsp cayenne pepper
- 1 tbsp olive oil
- 1/4 tsp paprika
- 1/8 tsp salt

Directions:

1. Preheat the Air Fryer to 390 F.
2. Add all ingredients into the bowl and toss well.
3. Transfer shrimp into the Air Fryer basket and cook for 6 minutes.
4. Serve and enjoy.

Tuna-Stuffed Potato Boats

Servings: 4
Cooking Time: 16 Minutes

Ingredients:

- 4 starchy potatoes, soaked for about 30 minutes and drain
- 1 (6-ounce) can tuna, drained
- 2 tablespoons plain Greek yogurt
- 1 scallion, chopped and divided
- 1 tablespoon capers
- ½ tablespoon olive oil
- 1 teaspoon red chili powder
- Salt and black pepper, to taste

Directions:

1. Preheat the Air Fryer to 355 o F and grease an Air Fryer basket.
2. Arrange the potatoes in the Air Fryer basket and cook for about 30 minutes.
3. Meanwhile, mix tuna, yogurt, red chili powder, salt, black pepper and half of scallion in a bowl and mash the mixture well.
4. Remove the potatoes from the Air Fryer and halve the potatoes lengthwise carefully.
5. Stuff in the tuna mixture in the potatoes and top with capers and remaining scallion.
6. Dish out in a platter and serve immediately.

Halibut Steaks With Vermouth And Herbs

Servings: 4
Cooking Time: 15 Minutes

Ingredients:

- 1 pound halibut steaks
- Salt and pepper, to your liking
- 1 teaspoon dried basil
- 2 tablespoons honey
- 1/4 cup vegetable oil
- 2 ½ tablespoons Worcester sauce
- 1 tablespoon freshly squeezed lemon juice
- 2 tablespoons vermouth
- 1 tablespoon fresh parsley leaves, coarsely chopped

Directions:

1. Place all the ingredients in a large-sized mixing dish. Gently stir to coat the fish evenly.
2. Set your Air Fryer to cook at 390 degrees F; roast for 5 minutes. Pause the machine and flip the fish over.
3. Then, cook for another 5 minutes; check for doneness and cook for a few more minutes as needed. Bon appétit!

Buttery Chives Trout

Servings: 4
Cooking Time: 12 Minutes

Ingredients:

- 4 trout fillets, boneless
- 4 tablespoons butter, melted
- Salt and black pepper to the taste
- Juice of 1 lime
- 1 tablespoon chives, chopped
- 1 tablespoon parsley, chopped

Directions:

1. Mix the fish fillets with the melted butter, salt and pepper, rub gently, put the fish in your Air Fryer's basket and cook at 390 degrees F for 6 minutes on each side.
2. Divide between plates and serve with lime juice drizzled on top and with parsley and chives sprinkled at the end.

Lemon And Oregano Tilapia Mix

Servings: 4
Cooking Time: 20 Minutes

Ingredients:

- 4 tilapia fillets, boneless and halved
- Salt and black pepper to the taste
- 1 cup roasted peppers, chopped
- ¼ cup keto tomato sauce
- 1 cup tomatoes, cubed
- 1 tablespoon lemon juice
- 2 tablespoons olive oil
- 1 teaspoon garlic powder
- 1 teaspoon oregano, dried

Directions:

1. In a baking dish that fits your Air Fryer, mix the fish with all the other ingredients, toss, introduce in your Air Fryer and cook at 380 degrees F for 20 minutes.
2. Divide into bowls and serve.

Italian Shrimp Scampi

Servings: 4
Cooking Time: 20 Minutes

Ingredients:

- 2 egg whites
- 1/2 cup coconut flour
- 1 cup Parmigiano-Reggiano, grated
- 1/2 teaspoon celery seeds
- 1/2 teaspoon porcini powder
- 1/2 teaspoon onion powder
- 1 teaspoon garlic powder
- 1/2 teaspoon dried rosemary
- 1/2 teaspoon sea salt
- 1/2 teaspoon ground black pepper
- 1 ½ pounds shrimp, deveined

Directions:

1. Whisk the egg with coconut flour and Parmigiano-Reggiano. Add in seasonings and mix to combine well.
2. Dip your shrimp in the batter. Roll until they are covered on all sides.
3. Cook in the preheated Air Fryer at 0 degrees F for 5 to 7 minutes or until golden brown. Work in batches.
4. Serve with lemon wedges if desired.

Sole Fish And Cauliflower Fritters

Servings: 2
Cooking Time: 30 Minutes

Ingredients:

- 1/2 pound sole fillets
- 1/2 pound mashed cauliflower
- 1 egg, well beaten
- 1/2 cup red onion, chopped
- 2 garlic cloves, minced
- 2 tablespoons fresh parsley, chopped
- 1 bell pepper, finely chopped
- 1/2 teaspoon scotch bonnet pepper, minced
- 1 tablespoon olive oil
- 1 tablespoon coconut aminos
- 1/2 teaspoon paprika
- Salt and white pepper, to taste

Directions:

1. Start by preheating your Air Fryer to 395 degrees F. Spritz the sides and bottom of the cooking basket with cooking spray.
2. Cook the sole fillets in the preheated Air Fryer for 10 minutes, flipping them halfway through the cooking time.
3. In a mixing bowl, mash the sole fillets into flakes. Stir in the remaining ingredients. Shape the fish mixture into patties.
4. Bake in the preheated Air Fryer at 390 degrees F for 1minutes, flipping them halfway through the cooking time. Bon appétit!

Flatten Salmon Balls

Servings: 2
Cooking Time: 13 Minutes

Ingredients:

- 4 tbsp celery, chopped
- 4 tbsp spring onion, sliced
- 4 tbsp wheat germ
- 4 tbsp olive oil
- 1 large egg
- 1 tbsp dill, fresh and chopped
- ½ tsp garlic powder

Directions:

1. Preheat the Air Fryer to 390 F. In a large bowl, mix the tinned salmon, egg, celery, onion, dill and garlic.
2. Shape the mixture into 2-inch size balls and roll them in wheat germ.
3. Heat the oil in a skillet and add the salmon balls; carefully flatten them.
4. Then place them in the air fryer and fry for 8 minutes.
5. Serve with yogurt or garlic mayo.

Tarragon Sea Bass And Risotto

Servings: 4
Cooking Time: 25 Minutes

Ingredients:

- 4 sea bass fillets, boneless
- A pinch of salt and black pepper
- 1 tablespoon ghee, melted
- 1 garlic clove, minced
- 1 cup cauliflower rice
- ½ cup chicken stock
- 1 tablespoon parmesan, grated
- 1 tablespoon chervil, chopped
- 1 tablespoon parsley, chopped
- 1 tablespoon tarragon, chopped

Directions:

1. In a pan that fits your Air Fryer, mix the cauliflower rice with the stock, parmesan, chervil, tarragon and parsley, toss, introduce the pan in the air fryer and cook at 380 degrees F for minutes.
2. In a bowl, mix the fish with salt, pepper, garlic and melted ghee and toss gently.
3. Put the fish over the cauliflower rice, cook at 380 degrees F for 12 minutes more, divide everything between plates and serve.

Parsley Shrimp

Servings: 4
Cooking Time: 12 Minutes

Ingredients:

- Pound shrimp, peeled and deveined
- 1 teaspoon cumin, ground
- 2 tablespoons parsley, chopped
- 2 tablespoons olive oil
- A pinch of salt and black pepper
- 4 garlic cloves, minced
- 1 tablespoon lime juice

Directions:

1. In a pan that fits your Air Fryer, mix all the ingredients, toss, put the pan in your Air Fryer and cook at 370 degrees F and cook for minutes, shaking the fryer halfway.
2. Divide into bowls and serve.

Lemony Tuna-Parsley Patties

Servings: 4
Cooking Time: 10 Minutes

Ingredients:

- ½ cup panko bread crumbs
- 1 egg, beaten
- 1 tablespoon lemon juice
- 2 cans of tuna in brine
- 2 tablespoons chopped parsley
- 2 teaspoons Dijon mustard
- 3 tablespoons olive oil
- A drizzle Tabasco sauce

Directions:

1. Drain the liquid from the canned tuna and put in a bowl.
2. Mix the tuna and season with mustard, bread crumbs, lemon juice, and parsley.
3. Add the egg and Tabasco sauce. Mix until well combined.
4. Form patties using your hands and place in the fried to set for at least 2 hours.
5. Preheat the Air Fryer to 3900F.
6. Place the grill pan accessory.
7. Brush the patties with olive oil and place on the grill pan.
8. Cook for 10 minutes.
9. Make sure to flip the patties halfway through the cooking time for even browning.

Lemon Shrimp

Servings: 2
Cooking Time: 8 Minutes

Ingredients:

- 12 oz shrimp, peeled and deveined
- 1 lemon sliced
- 1/4 tsp garlic powder
- 1/4 tsp paprika
- 1 tsp lemon pepper
- 1 lemon juice
- 1 tbsp olive oil

Directions:

1. In a bowl, mix together oil, lemon juice, garlic powder, paprika, and lemon pepper.
2. Add shrimp to the bowl and toss well to coat.
3. Spray Air Fryer basket with cooking spray.
4. Transfer shrimp into the Air Fryer basket and cook at 0 F for 8 minutes.
5. Garnish with lemon slices and serve.

Ham-Wrapped Prawns With Roasted Pepper Chutney

Servings: 4
Cooking Time: 13 Minutes

Ingredients:

- 1 large red bell pepper
- 8 king prawns, peeled and deveined
- 4 ham slices, halved
- 1 garlic clove, minced
- 1 tablespoon olive oil
- ½ tablespoon paprika
- Salt and freshly ground black pepper, to taste

Directions:

1. Preheat the Air Fryer to 375 o F and grease an Air Fryer basket.
2. Place the bell pepper in the Air Fryer basket and cook for about 10 minutes.
3. Dish out the bell pepper into a bowl and keep aside, covered for about 15 minutes.
4. Now, peel the bell pepper and remove the stems and seeds and chop it.
5. Put the chopped bell pepper, garlic, paprika and olive oil in a blender and pulse until a puree is formed.
6. Wrap each ham slice around each prawn and transfer to the Air Fryer basket.
7. Cook for about 3 minutes and serve with roasted pepper chutney.

Herbed Garlic Lobster

Servings: 3
Cooking Time: 15 Minutes

Ingredients:

- 1 tsp garlic, minced
- 1 tbsp butter
- Salt and pepper to taste
- ½ tbsp lemon Juice

Directions:

1. Add all the ingredients to a food processor, except shrimp, and blend well.
2. Clean the skin of the lobster and cover with the marinade.
3. Preheat your Air Fryer to 380 F.
4. Place the lobster in your Air Fryer's cooking basket and cook for minutes.
5. Serve with fresh herbs and enjoy!

Spiced Coco Lime Skewered Shrimp

Servings: 6
Cooking Time: 12 Minutes

Ingredients:

- 1 lime, zested and juiced
- 1/3 cup chopped fresh cilantro
- 1/3 cup shredded coconut
- 1/4 cup olive oil
- 1/4 cup soy sauce
- 1-pound uncooked medium shrimp, peeled and deveined
- 2 garlic cloves
- 2 jalapeno peppers, seeded

Directions:

1. In food processor, process until smooth the soy sauce, olive oil, coconut oil, cilantro, garlic, lime juice, lime zest, and jalapeno.
2. In a shallow dish, mix well shrimp and processed marinade. Toss well to coat and marinate in the ref for 3 hours.
3. Thread shrimps in skewers. Place on skewer rack in Air Fryer.
4. For 6 minutes, cook on 360oF. If needed, cook in batches.
5. Serve and enjoy.

Rosemary Garlic Prawns

Servings: 2
Cooking Time: 15 Minutes

Ingredients:

- 3 garlic cloves, minced
- 1 rosemary sprig, chopped
- ½ tbsp melted butter
- Salt and pepper, to taste

Directions:

1. Combine garlic, butter, rosemary, salt and pepper, in a bowl.
2. Add the prawns to the bowl and mix to coat them well.
3. Cover the bowl and refrigerate for an hour.
4. Preheat the Air Fryer to 350 F, and cook for 6 minutes.
5. Increase the temperature to 390 degrees, and cook for one more minute.

Salmon With Broccoli

Servings: 2
Cooking Time: 12 Minutes

Ingredients:

- 1½ cups small broccoli florets
- ¼ teaspoon cornstarch
- 2 (6-ounces) salmon fillets, skin-on
- 1 scallion, thinly sliced
- 2 tablespoons vegetable oil, divided
- Salt and black pepper, as required
- 1 (½-inch) piece fresh ginger, grated
- 1 tablespoon soy sauce
- 1 teaspoon rice vinegar
- 1 teaspoon light brown sugar

Directions:

1. Preheat the Air Fryer to 375 o F and grease an Air Fryer basket.
2. Mix the broccoli, 1 tablespoon of vegetable oil, salt, and black pepper.
3. Combine ginger, soy sauce, rice vinegar, sugar and cornstarch in another bowl.
4. Rub the salmon fillets evenly with remaining olive oil and the ginger mixture.
5. Place the broccoli florets into the Air Fryer basket and top with salmon fillets.
6. Cook for about 12 minutes and dish out in serving plates.

Italian Sardinas Fritas

Servings: 4
Cooking Time: 1 Hour 15 Minutes

Ingredients:

- ½ pounds sardines, cleaned and rinsed
- Salt and ground black pepper, to savor
- 1 tablespoon Italian seasoning mix
- 1 tablespoon lemon juice
- 1 tablespoon soy sauce
- 2 tablespoons olive oil

Directions:

1. Firstly, pat the sardines dry with a kitchen towel. Add salt, black pepper, Italian seasoning mix, lemon juice, soy sauce, and olive oil; marinate them for 30 minutes.
2. Air-fry the sardines at 350 degrees F for approximately 5 minutes.
3. Increase the temperature to 385 degrees F and air-fry them for further 7 to 8 minutes.
4. Then, place the sardines in a nice serving platter. Bon appétit!

Hot Tilapia

Servings: 2
Cooking Time: 9 Minutes

Ingredients:

- 1 chili pepper, chopped
- 1 teaspoon chili flakes
- 1 tablespoon sesame oil
- ½ teaspoon salt 10 oz tilapia fillet
- ¼ teaspoon onion powder

Directions:

1. In the shallow bowl mix up chili pepper, chili flakes, salt, and onion powder.
2. Gently churn the mixture and add sesame oil.
3. After this, slice the tilapia fillet and sprinkle with chili mixture. Massage the fish with the help of the fingertips gently and leave for minutes to marinate.
4. Preheat the Air Fryer to 390F.
5. Put the tilapia fillets in the Air Fryer basket and cook for 5 minutes.
6. Then flip the fish on another side and cook for 4 minutes more.

Rich Crab Croquettes

Servings: 4
Cooking Time: 30 Minutes

Ingredients:

- 1 ½ lb lump crab meat
- 3 egg whites, beaten
- 1/3 cup sour cream
- 1/3 cup mayonnaise
- 1 ½ tbsp olive oil
- 1 red pepper, chopped finely
- 1/3 cup chopped red onion
- 2 ½ tbsp chopped celery
- ½ tsp chopped tarragon
- ½ tsp chopped chives
- 1 tsp chopped parsley
- 1 tsp cayenne pepper Breading:
- 1 ½ cup breadcrumbs
- 2 tsp olive oil
- 1 cup flour
- 4 eggs, beaten
- Salt to taste

Directions:

1. Place a skillet over medium heat on a stovetop, add ½ tbsp olive oil, red pepper, onion, and celery. Sauté for 5 minutes or until sweaty and translucent. Turn off heat.
2. Add the breadcrumbs, the remaining olive oil, and salt to a food processor. Blend to mix evenly; set aside.
3. In 2 separate bowls, add the flour and 4 eggs respectively, set aside.
4. In a separate bowl, add crabmeat, mayo, egg whites, sour cream, tarragon, chives, parsley, cayenne pepper, and celery sauté and mix evenly.
5. Form bite-sized balls from the mixture and place onto a plate.
6. Preheat the Air Fryer to 0 F. Dip each crab meatball (croquettes) in the egg mixture and press them in the breadcrumb mixture. Place the croquettes in the fryer basket, avoid overcrowding. Close the Air Fryer and cook for 10 minutes or until golden brown. Remove them and plate them.
7. Serve the crab croquettes with tomato dipping sauce and a side of vegetable fries.

Crab Herb Croquettes

Servings: 6
Cooking Time: 30 Minutes

Ingredients:

- 1 lb. crab meat
- 1 cup friendly bread crumbs
- 2 egg whites
- ½ tsp. parsley
- ¼ tsp. chives
- ¼ tsp. tarragon
- 2 tbsp. celery, chopped
- ¼ cup red pepper, chopped
- 1 tsp. olive oil
- ½ tsp. lime juice
- 4 tbsp. sour cream
- 4 tbsp. mayonnaise
- ¼ cup onion, chopped
- ¼ tsp. salt

Directions:

1. Put the bread crumbs and salt in a bowl.
2. Pour the egg whites in a separate bowl.
3. Place the rest of the ingredients in a third bowl and combine thoroughly.
4. Using your hands, shape equal amounts of the mixture into small balls and dredge each ball in the egg white before coating with the bread crumbs.
5. Put the croquettes in the Air Fryer basket and cook at 400°F for 18 minutes. Serve hot.

Cajun Shrimp

Servings: 4
Cooking Time: 25 Minutes

Ingredients:

- ¼ tsp. cayenne pepper
- ¼ tsp. smoked paprika
- ½ tsp. old bay seasoning
- 1 tbsp. olive oil
- Pinch of salt
- 1 ¼ lb. tiger shrimp

Directions:

1. Pre-heat your Air Fryer to 390°F.
2. In a large bowl, combine together all the ingredients, ensuring to coat the shrimps well.
3. Transfer to the fryer and cook for 5 minutes.
4. Serve over boiled rice.

Tilapia Bowls

Servings: 4
Cooking Time: 10 Minutes

Ingredients:

- 7 oz tilapia fillet or flathead fish
- 1 teaspoon arrowroot powder
- 1 teaspoon ground paprika
- ½ teaspoon salt
- ½ teaspoon ground black pepper
- ¼ teaspoon ground cumin
- ½ teaspoon garlic powder
- 1 teaspoon lemon juice
- 4 oz purple cabbage, shredded
- 1 jalapeno, sliced
- 1 tablespoon heavy cream
- ½ teaspoon minced garlic
- Cooking spray

Directions:

1. Sprinkle the tilapia fillet with arrowroot powder, ground paprika, salt, ground black pepper, ground cumin, and garlic powder.
2. Preheat the Air Fryer to 385F.
3. Spray the tilapia fillet with cooking spray and place it in the Air Fryer.
4. Cook the fish for minutes.
5. Meanwhile, in the bowl mix up shredded cabbage, jalapeno pepper, and lemon juice.
6. When the tilapia fillet is cooked, chop it roughly.
7. Put the shredded cabbage mixture in the serving bowls. Top them with chopped tilapia.
8. After this, in the shallow bowl mix up minced garlic and heavy cream.
9. Sprinkle the meal with a heavy cream mixture.

Halibut Steaks

Servings: 4
Cooking Time: 15 Minutes

Ingredients:

- 1 lb. halibut steaks
- Salt and pepper to taste
- 1 tsp. dried basil
- 2 tbsp. honey
- ¼ cup vegetable oil
- 2 ½ tbsp. Worcester sauce
- 1 tbsp. freshly squeezed lemon juice
- 2 tbsp. vermouth
- 1 tbsp. fresh parsley leaves, coarsely chopped

Directions:

1. Put all of the ingredients in a large bowl. Combine and cover the fish completely with the seasoning.
2. Transfer to your Air Fryer and cook at 390°F for 5 minutes.
3. Turn the fish over and allow to cook for a further 5 minutes.
4. Ensure the fish is cooked through, leaving it in the fryer for a few more minutes if necessary.
5. Serve with a side of potato salad.

Easy Creamy Shrimp Nachos

Servings: 4

Cooking Time: 15 Minutes

Ingredients:

- 1 pound shrimp, cleaned and deveined
- 1 tablespoon olive oil
- 2 tablespoons fresh lemon juice
- 1 teaspoon paprika
- 1/4 teaspoon cumin powder
- 1/2 teaspoon shallot powder
- 1/2 teaspoon garlic powder
- Coarse sea salt and ground black pepper, to taste
- 1 (9-ounce) bag corn tortilla chips
- 1/4 cup pickled jalapeño, minced
- 1 cup Pepper Jack cheese, grated
- 1/2 cup sour cream

Directions:

1. Toss the shrimp with the olive oil, lemon juice, paprika, cumin powder, shallot powder, garlic powder, salt, and black pepper.
2. Cook in the preheated Air Fryer at 390 degrees F for 5 minutes.
3. Place the tortilla chips on the aluminum foil-lined cooking basket. Top with the shrimp mixture, jalapeño and cheese. Cook another 2 minutes or until cheese has melted.
4. Serve garnished with sour cream and enjoy!

Poultry Recipes

Prune-Stuffed Turkey Tenderloins

Servings: 4
Cooking Time: 1 Hour

Ingredients:

- 3/4 cup prunes, pitted and chopped
- 1/2 teaspoon dried marjoram
- 1 sprig thyme, leaves only, crushed
- 2 tablespoons fresh coriander, minced
- 1/4 teaspoon ground allspice
- 1/2 cup softened butter
- 1 ½ pounds turkey tenderloins
- 2 tablespoons dry white wine

Directions:

1. In a mixing bowl, thoroughly combine the first 6 ingredients; stir with a spoon until everything is well shared.
2. Cut the "pockets" into the sides of the turkey tenderloins. Stuff them with prepared prune mixture. Now, tie each "pocket" with a cooking twine. Sprinkle them with white wine.
3. Cook the stuffed turkey in the preheated Air Fryer at 5 degrees F for 48 to 55 minutes, checking periodically.
4. Afterward, remove cooking twine, cut each turkey tenderloin into 2 slices and serve immediately.

Sweet and Sour Chicken Thighs

Servings: 2
Cooking Time: 20 Minutes

Ingredients:

- 1 scallion, finely chopped
- 1 garlic clove, minced
- ½ tablespoon soy sauce
- ½ tablespoon rice vinegar
- 1 teaspoon sugar
- Salt and ground black pepper, as required
- 2 (4-ounces) skinless, boneless chicken thighs
- ½ cup corn flour

Directions:

1. Mix together all the ingredients except chicken, and corn flour in a bowl.
2. Add the chicken thighs and generously coat with marinade.
3. Add the corn flour in another bowl.
4. Remove the chicken thighs from marinade and coat with corn flour.
5. Set the temperature of Air Fryer to 390 degrees F. Grease an Air Fryer basket.
6. Arrange chicken thighs into the prepared Air Fryer basket, skin side down.
7. Air Fry for about 10 minutes and then another 10 minutes at 355 degrees F.
8. Remove from Air Fryer and transfer the chicken thighs onto a serving platter.
9. Serve hot.

Oregano And Lemon Chicken Drumsticks

Servings: 4
Cooking Time: 21 Minutes

Ingredients:

- 4 chicken drumsticks, with skin, bone-in
- 1 teaspoon dried cilantro
- ½ teaspoon dried oregano
- ½ teaspoon salt
- 1 teaspoon lemon juice
- 1 teaspoon butter, softened
- 2 garlic cloves, diced

Directions:

1. In the mixing bowl mix up dried cilantro, oregano, and salt.
2. Then fill the chicken drumstick's skin with a cilantro mixture. Add butter and diced garlic. Sprinkle the chicken with lemon juice.
3. Preheat the Air Fryer to 375F.
4. Put the chicken drumsticks in the Air Fryer and cook them for 2 minutes.

Paprika-Cumin Rubbed Chicken Tenderloin

Servings: 6
Cooking Time: 25 Minutes

Ingredients:

- ¼ cup coconut flour
- ¼ cup olive oil
- ½ teaspoon garlic powder
- ½ teaspoon ground cumin
- ½ teaspoon onion powder
- ½ teaspoon smoked paprika
- 1-pound chicken tenderloins
- Salt and pepper to taste

Directions:

1. Preheat the air fryer for 5 minutes.
2. Soak the chicken tenderloins in olive oil.
3. Mix the rest of the ingredients and stir using your hands to combine everything.
4. Place the chicken pieces in the Air Fryer basket.
5. Cook for 2 minutes at 3250F. Serve hot.

Air Fried Southern Drumsticks

Servings: 4
Cooking Time: 50 Minutes

Ingredients:

- 2 tbsp oregano
- 2 tbsp thyme
- 2 oz oats
- ¼ cup milk
- ¼ steamed cauliflower florets
- 1 egg
- 1 tbsp ground cayenne
- Salt and pepper, to taste

Directions:

1. Preheat the air fryer to 350 F and season the drumsticks with salt and pepper; rub them with the milk. Place all the other ingredients, except the egg, in a food processor. Process until smooth.
2. Dip each drumstick in the egg first, and then in the oat mixture. Arrange half of them on a baking mat inside the Air Fryer. Cook for minutes. Repeat with the other batch.

Parmesan And Dill Chicken

Servings: 6
Cooking Time: 20 Minutes

Ingredients:

- 18 oz chicken breast, skinless, boneless
- 5 oz pork rinds
- 3 oz Parmesan, grated
- 3 eggs, beaten
- 1 teaspoon chili flakes
- 1 teaspoon ground paprika
- 2 tablespoons avocado oil
- 1 teaspoon Erythritol
- ¼ teaspoon onion powder
- 1 teaspoon cayenne pepper
- 1 chili pepper, minced
- ½ teaspoon dried dill

Directions:

1. In the shallow bowl mix up chili flakes, ground paprika, Erythritol. Onion powder, and cayenne pepper. Add dried dill and stir the mixture gently.
2. Then rub the chicken breast in the spice mixture.
3. Then rub the chicken with minced chili pepper. Dip the chicken breast in the beaten eggs.
4. After this, coat it in the Parmesan and dip in the eggs again.
5. Then coat the chicken in the pork rinds and sprinkle with avocado oil.
6. Preheat the Air Fryer to 380F.
7. Put the chicken breast in the Air Fryer and cook it for minutes. Then flip the chicken breast on another side and cook it for 4 minutes more.

Citrus Turkey Legs

Servings: 2

Cooking Time: 30 Minutes + Marinate Time

Ingredients:

- 1 tablespoon fresh rosemary, minced
- 2 turkey legs
- 2 garlic cloves, minced
- 1 teaspoon fresh lime zest, finely grated
- 2 tablespoons olive oil
- 1 tablespoon fresh lime juice
- Salt and black pepper, as required

Directions:

1. Preheat the Air Fryer to 350 o F and grease an Air fryer basket.
2. Mix the garlic, rosemary, lime zest, oil, lime juice, salt, and black pepper in a bowl.
3. Coat the turkey legs with marinade and refrigerate to marinate for about 8 hours.
4. Arrange the turkey legs into the Air Fryer basket and cook for about 30 minutes, flipping once in between.
5. Dish out the turkey legs into serving plates.

Fried Chicken Thighs

Servings: 4
Cooking Time: 35 Minutes

Ingredients:

- 4 chicken thighs
- 1 ½ tbsp. Cajun seasoning
- 1 egg, beaten
- ½ cup flour
- 1 tsp. seasoning salt

Directions:

1. Pre-heat the Air Fryer to 350°F.
2. In a bowl combine the flour, Cajun seasoning, and seasoning salt.
3. Place the beaten egg in another bowl.
4. Coat the chicken with the flour before dredging it in the egg. Roll once more in the flour.
5. Put the chicken in the Air Fryer and cook for 2 minutes. Serve hot.

Paprika Duck

Servings: 6
Cooking Time: 28 Minutes

Ingredients:

- 10 oz duck skin
- 1 teaspoon sunflower oil
- ½ teaspoon salt
- ½ teaspoon ground paprika

Directions:

1. Preheat the Air Fryer to 375F.
2. Then sprinkle the duck skin with sunflower oil, salt, and ground paprika. Put the duck skin in the Air Fryer and cook it for minutes.
3. Then flip it on another side and cook for 10 minutes more or until it is crunchy from both sides.

Paprika Chicken Legs With Turnip

Servings: 3
Cooking Time: 30 Minutes

Ingredients:

- 1 pound chicken legs
- 1 teaspoon Himalayan salt
- 1 teaspoon paprika
- 1/2 teaspoon ground black pepper
- 1 teaspoon butter, melted
- 1 turnip, trimmed and sliced

Directions:

1. Spritz the sides and bottom of the cooking basket with a nonstick cooking spray.
2. Season the chicken legs with salt, paprika, and ground black pepper.
3. Cook at 0 degrees F for 10 minutes. Increase the temperature to 380 degrees F.
4. Drizzle turnip slices with melted butter and transfer them to the cooking basket with the chicken. Cook the turnips and chicken for 15 minutes more, flipping them halfway through the cooking time.
5. As for the chicken, an instant-read thermometer should read at least 16 degrees F.
6. Serve and enjoy!

Cauliflower Stuffed Chicken

Servings: 5
Cooking Time: 25 Minutes

Ingredients:

- 1 ½-pound chicken breast, skinless, boneless
- ½ cup cauliflower, shredded
- 1 jalapeno pepper, chopped
- 1 teaspoon ground nutmeg
- 1 teaspoon salt
- ¼ cup Cheddar cheese, shredded
- ½ teaspoon cayenne pepper
- 1 tablespoon cream cheese
- 1 tablespoon sesame oil
- ½ teaspoon dried thyme

Directions:

1. Make the horizontal cut in the chicken breast.
2. In the mixing bowl mix up shredded cauliflower, chopped jalapeno pepper, ground nutmeg, salt, and cayenne pepper.
3. Fill the chicken cut with the shredded cauliflower and secure the cut with toothpicks.
4. Then rub the chicken breast with cream cheese, dried thyme, and sesame oil.
5. Preheat the Air Fryer to 380F.
6. Put the chicken breast in the Air Fryer and cook it for 20 minutes.
7. Then sprinkle it with Cheddar cheese and cook for 5 minutes more.

Piri Piri Chicken

Servings: 6
Cooking Time: 1 Hour 30 Minutes

Ingredients:

- 12 chicken wings
- 1 ½ ounces butter, melted
- 1 teaspoon onion powder
- 1/2 teaspoon cumin powder
- 1 teaspoon garlic paste

For the Sauce:

- 2 ounces piri piri peppers, stemmed and chopped
- 1 tablespoon pimiento, deveined and minced
- 1 garlic clove, chopped
- 2 tablespoons fresh lemon juice
- 1/3 teaspoon sea salt
- 1/2 teaspoon tarragon

Directions:

1. Steam the chicken wings using a steamer basket that is placed over a saucepan with boiling water; reduce the heat.
2. Now, steam the wings for 10 minutes over a moderate heat. Toss the wings with butter, onion powder, cumin powder, and garlic paste.
3. Let the chicken wings cool to room temperature. Then, refrigerate them for 45 to 50 minutes.
4. Roast in the preheated Air Fryer at 330 degrees F for 25 to 30 minutes; make sure to flip them halfway through.
5. While the chicken wings are cooking, prepare the sauce by mixing all of the sauce ingredients in a food processor. Toss the wings with prepared Piri Piri Sauce and serve.

Easy How-To Hard Boil Egg In Air Fryer

Servings: 6

Cooking Time: 15 Minutes

Ingredients:

- 6 eggs

Directions:

1. Preheat the Air Fryer for 5 minutes.
2. Place the eggs in the Air Fryer basket.
3. Cook for 15 minutes at 00F.
4. Remove from the Air Fryer basket and place in cold water.

Portuguese Roasted Whole Chicken

Servings: 4
Cooking Time: 50 Minutes

Ingredients:

- Salt and pepper to season
- 1 tbsp chili powder
- 1 tbsp garlic powder
- 4 tbsp oregano
- 2 tbsp coriander powder
- 2 tbsp cumin powder
- 2 tbsp olive oil
- 4 tbsp paprika
- 1 lime, juiced

Directions:

1. Rub the salmon with dried rosemary and salt.
2. In a bowl, pour oregano, garlic powder, chili powder, ground coriander, paprika, cumin powder, pepper, salt, and olive oil.
3. Mix well to create a rub for the chicken, and rub onto it. Refrigerate for 20 minutes.
4. Preheat Air Fryer to 350 F. Remove the chicken from the refrigerator; place in the fryer basket and cook for minutes. Use a skewer to poke the chicken to ensure that is clear of juices.
5. Let to rest for 10 minutes.
6. After, drizzle the lime juice over and serve.

Lemon Pepper Chicken Legs

Servings: 4
Cooking Time: 30 Minutes

Ingredients:

- ½ tsp. garlic powder
- 2 tsp. baking powder
- 8 chicken legs
- 4 tbsp. salted butter, melted
- 1 tbsp. lemon pepper seasoning

Directions:

1. In a small bowl combine the garlic powder and baking powder, then use this mixture to coat the chicken legs. Lay the chicken in the basket of your fryer.
2. Cook the chicken legs at 375°F for twenty-five minutes. Halfway through, turn them over and allow to cook on the other side.
3. When the chicken has turned golden brown, test with a thermometer to ensure it has reached an ideal temperature of 165°F. Remove from the Fryer.
4. Mix together the melted butter and lemon pepper seasoning and toss with the chicken legs until the chicken is coated all over. Serve hot.

Turkey Wings

Servings: 4
Cooking Time: 26 Minutes

Ingredients:

- 2 pounds turkey wings
- 4 tablespoons chicken rub
- 3 tablespoons olive oil

Directions:

1. In a large bowl, mix together the turkey wings, chicken rub, and oil using your hands.
2. Set the temperature of Air Fryer to 380 degrees F. Grease an Air Fryer basket.
3. Arrange turkey wings into the prepared Air Fryer basket.
4. Air Fry for about 26 minutes, flipping once halfway through.
5. Remove from Air Fryer and place the turkey wings onto the serving plates.
6. Serve hot.

Spiced Chicken Breasts

Servings: 4
Cooking Time: 23 Minutes

Ingredients:

- 2 tablespoons butter, melted
- 4 (6-ounces) boneless, skinless chicken breasts
- ¼ teaspoon garlic powder
- ¼ teaspoon onion powder
- ¼ teaspoon smoked paprika
- Salt and black pepper, as required

Directions:

1. Preheat the Air Fryer to 350 o F and grease an Air Fryer basket.
2. Mix butter and spices in a bowl and coat the chicken with this mixture.
3. Transfer into the Air Fryer and cook for about 2minutes, flipping once in between.
4. Dish out the chicken into a serving platter and serve hot.

Crispy Chicken Drumsticks

Servings: 2
Cooking Time: 20 Minutes

Ingredients:

- 4 (4-ounces) chicken drumsticks
- ½ cup buttermilk
- ½ cup all-purpose flour
- ½ cup panko breadcrumbs
- 3 tablespoons butter, melted
- ¼ teaspoon baking powder
- ¼ teaspoon dried oregano
- ¼ teaspoon dried thyme
- ¼ teaspoon celery salt
- ¼ teaspoon garlic powder
- ¼ teaspoon ground ginger
- ¼ teaspoon cayenne pepper
- ¼ teaspoon paprika
- Salt and ground black pepper, as required

Directions:

1. Preheat the Air Fryer to 390 o F and grease an Air Fryer basket.
2. Put the chicken drumsticks and buttermilk in a resealable plastic bag.
3. Seal the bag tightly and refrigerate for about hours.
4. Mix the flour, breadcrumbs, baking powder, herbs and spices in a bowl.
5. Remove the chicken drumsticks from bag and coat chicken drumsticks evenly with the seasoned flour mixture.
6. Transfer the chicken drumsticks into the Air Fryer basket and cook for about 20 minutes, flipping once in between.
7. Dish out and serve hot.

Air Fried Chicken Fillets With Coconut Rice

Servings: 4
Cooking Time: 15 Minutes

Ingredients:

- 4 (4-ounce) skinless, boneless chicken breasts
- 2¼ cups water
- 1 (14-ounce) can coconut milk
- 1 cup rice
- ½ cup coconut cream
- 1 garlic clove, minced
- 1 teaspoon fresh lime zest, grated finely
- 3 teaspoons avocado oil
- 2 tablespoons fresh lime juice
- 2 teaspoons soy sauce
- 2 teaspoons pure maple syrup
- ¼ teaspoon chile paste
- 2 teaspoons curry powder
- 1½ teaspoons ground coriander
- 1 teaspoon ground cumin
- ¼ teaspoons dried cilantro, crushed
- Pinch of cayenne pepper
- Salt, to taste

Directions:

1. Preheat the Air Fryer to 370 o F and grease an Air Fryer basket.
2. Put all the ingredients in a large bowl except chicken and mix until well combined.
3. Stir in the chicken and coat generously with marinade.
4. Cover the bowl and refrigerate for about 2hours.
5. Arrange the chicken in the Air Fryer basket and cook for about 1minutes.
6. Meanwhile, mix water, coconut cream, rice and salt in a pan and bring to a boil.
7. Lower the heat, cover and let it simmer for about 15 minutes.
8. Serve chicken with coconut rice.

Coconut Turkey And Spinach Mix

Servings: 4
Cooking Time: 15 Minutes

Ingredients:

- 1 pound turkey meat, ground and browned
- 1 tablespoon garlic, minced
- 1 tablespoon ginger, grated
- 2 tablespoons coconut aminos
- 4 cups spinach leaves
- A pinch of salt and black pepper

Directions:

1. In a pan that fits your Air Fryer, combine all the ingredients and toss.
2. Put the pan in the Air Fryer and cook at 380 degrees F for minutes.
3. Divide everything into bowls and serve.

Lime And Mustard Marinated Chicken

Servings: 4

Cooking Time: 30 Minutes + Marinating Time

Ingredients:

- 1/2 teaspoon stone-ground mustard
- 1/2 teaspoon minced fresh oregano
- 1/3 cup freshly squeezed lime juice
- 2 small-sized chicken breasts, skin-on
- 1 teaspoon kosher salt
- 1teaspoon freshly cracked mixed peppercorns

Directions:

1. Preheat your Air Fryer to 345 degrees F.
2. Toss all of the above ingredients in a medium-sized mixing dish; allow it to marinate overnight.
3. Cook in the preheated Air Fryer for 26 minutes. Bon appétit!

Duck Breast With Fig Sauce Recipe

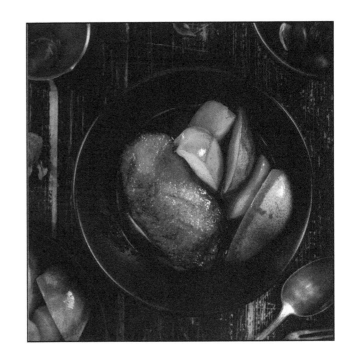

Servings: 4
Cooking Time: 30 Minutes

Ingredients:

- 2 duck breasts; skin on, halved
- 1 tbsp. white flour
- 1 tbsp. olive oil
- 1/2 tsp. thyme; chopped
- 1/2 cup port wine
- 1/2 tsp. garlic powder
- 1/4 tsp. sweet paprika
- 1 cup beef stock
- 3 tbsp. butter; melted
- 1 shallot; chopped
- 4 tbsp. fig preserves
- Salt and black pepper to the taste

Directions:

1. Season duck breasts with salt and pepper, drizzle half of the melted butter, rub well, put in your Air Fryer's basket and cook at 350 °F, for 5 minutes on each side.
2. Meanwhile; heat up a pan with the olive oil and the rest of the butter over medium high heat, add shallot; stir and cook for minutes.
3. Add thyme, garlic powder, paprika, stock, salt, pepper, wine and figs; stir and cook for 7-8 minutes.
4. Add flour; stir well, cook until sauce thickens a bit and take off heat.
5. Divide duck breasts on plates, drizzle figs sauce all over and serve.

Surprisingly Tasty Chicken

Servings: 4
Cooking Time: 1 Hour

Ingredients:

- 1 (1½ pound) whole chicken
- 1 pound small potatoes
- Salt and black pepper, to taste
- 1 tablespoon olive oil, scrubbed

Directions:

1. Preheat the Air Fryer to 390 o F and grease an Air Fryer basket.
2. Season the chicken with salt and black pepper and transfer into the Air Fryer.
3. Cook for about 40 minutes and dish out in a plate, covering with a foil paper.
4. Mix potato, oil, salt and black pepper in a bowl and toss to coat well.
5. Arrange the potatoes into the Air Fryer basket and cook for 20 minutes.
6. Dish out and serve warm.

Chicken Sausage In Dijon Sauce

Servings: 4
Cooking Time: 20 Minutes

Ingredients:

- 4 chicken sausages
- 1/4 cup mayonnaise
- 2 tablespoons Dijon mustard
- 1 tablespoon balsamic vinegar
- 1/2 teaspoon dried rosemary

Directions:

1. Arrange the sausages on the grill pan and transfer it to the preheated Air Fryer.
2. Grill the sausages at 350 degrees F for approximately 13 minutes. Turn them halfway through cooking.
3. Meanwhile, prepare the sauce by mixing the remaining ingredients with a wire whisk. Serve the warm sausages with chilled Dijon sauce. Enjoy!

Duck Breasts With Candy Onion And Coriander

Servings: 4
Cooking Time: 25 Minutes

Ingredients:

- 1 ½ pounds duck breasts, skin removed
- 1 teaspoon kosher salt
- 1/2 teaspoon cayenne pepper
- 1/3 teaspoon black pepper
- 1/2 teaspoon smoked paprika
- 1 tablespoon Thai red curry paste
- 1 cup candy onions, halved
- 1/4 small pack coriander, chopped

Directions:

1. Place the duck breasts between 2 sheets of foil; then, use a rolling pin to bash the duck until they are inch thick.
2. Preheat your Air Fryer to 395 degrees F.
3. Rub the duck breasts with salt, cayenne pepper, black pepper, paprika, and red curry paste. Place the duck breast in the cooking basket.
4. Cook for 11 to 12 minutes. Top with candy onions and cook for another 10 to 11 minutes.
5. Serve garnished with coriander and enjoy!

Parmesan Chicken Cutlets

Servings: 4
Cooking Time: 30 Minutes

Ingredients:

- ¾ cup all-purpose flour
- 2 large eggs
- 1½ cups panko breadcrumbs
- ¼ cup Parmesan cheese, grated
- 4 (6-ounces) (¼-inch thick) skinless, boneless chicken cutlets
- 1 tablespoon mustard powder
- Salt and black pepper, to taste

Directions:

1. Preheat the Air Fryer to 355 o F and grease an Air Fryer basket.
2. Place the flour in a shallow bowl and whisk the eggs in a second bowl.
3. Mix the breadcrumbs, cheese, mustard powder, salt, and black pepper in a third bowl.
4. Season the chicken with salt and black pepper and coat the chicken with flour.
5. Dip the chicken into whisked eggs and finally dredge into the breadcrumb mixture.
6. Arrange the chicken cutlets into the Air Fryer basket and cook for about 30 minutes.
7. Dish out in a platter and immediately serve.

Cheddar Garlic Turkey

Servings: 4
Cooking Time: 20 Minutes

Ingredients:

- 1 big turkey breast, skinless, boneless and cubed
- Salt and black pepper to the taste
- ¼ cup cheddar cheese, grated
- ¼ teaspoon garlic powder
- 1 tablespoon olive oil

Directions:

1. Rub the turkey cubes with the oil, season with salt, pepper and garlic powder and dredge in cheddar cheese.
2. Put the turkey bits in your Air Fryer's basket and cook at 380 degrees F for 20 minutes.
3. Divide between plates and serve with a side salad.
4.

Cheese Herb Chicken Wings

Servings: 4
Cooking Time: 15 Minutes

Ingredients:

- 2 lbs chicken wings
- 1 tsp herb de Provence
- ½ cup parmesan cheese, grated
- 1 tsp paprika
- Salt

Directions:

1. Preheat the Air Fryer to 350 F.
2. In a small bowl, mix together cheese, herb de Provence, paprika, and salt.
3. Spray Air Fryer basket with cooking spray.
4. Toss chicken wings with cheese mixture and place into the Air Fryer basket and cook for 15 minutes. Turn halfway through.
5. Serve and enjoy.

Lemon And Chili Chicken Drumsticks

Servings: 6
Cooking Time: 20 Minutes

Ingredients:

- 6 chicken drumsticks
- 1 teaspoon dried oregano
- 1 tablespoon lemon juice
- ½ teaspoon lemon zest, grated
- 1 teaspoon ground cumin
- ½ teaspoon chili flakes
- 1 teaspoon garlic powder
- ½ teaspoon ground coriander
- 1 tablespoon avocado oil

Directions:

1. Rub the chicken drumsticks with dried oregano, lemon juice, lemon zest, ground cumin, chili flakes, garlic powder, and ground coriander.
2. Then sprinkle them with avocado oil and put in the Air Fryer.
3. Cook the chicken drumsticks for 20 minutes at 375F.

Chicken And Chickpeas Mix

Servings: 4
Cooking Time: 25 Minutes

Ingredients:

- 5 ounces bacon, cooked and crumbled
- 2 tablespoons olive oil
- 1 cup yellow onion, chopped
- 8 ounces canned chickpeas, drained
- 2 carrots, chopped
- 1 tablespoon parsley, chopped
- Salt and black pepper to taste
- 2 pounds chicken thighs, boneless
- 1 cup chicken stock
- 1 teaspoon balsamic vinegar

Directions:

1. Heat up a pan that fits your Air Fryer with the oil over medium heat.
2. Add the onions, carrots, salt and pepper; stir, and sauté for 3-4 minutes.
3. Add the chicken, stock, vinegar, and chickpeas; then toss.
4. Place the pan in the fryer and cook at 380 degrees F for 20 minutes.
5. Add the bacon and the parsley and toss again.
6. Divide everything between plates and serve.

Almond Flour Coco-Milk Battered Chicken

Servings: 4
Cooking Time: 30 Minutes

Ingredients:

- ¼ cup coconut milk
- ½ cup almond flour
- 1 ½ tablespoons old bay Cajun seasoning
- 1 egg, beaten
- 4 small chicken thighs
- Salt and pepper to taste

Directions:

1. Preheat the Air Fryer for 5 minutes.
2. Mix the egg and coconut milk in a bowl.
3. Soak the chicken thighs in the beaten egg mixture.
4. In a mixing bowl, combine the almond flour, Cajun seasoning, salt and pepper.
5. Dredge the chicken thighs in the almond flour mixture.
6. Place in the Air Fryer basket.
7. Cook for 30 minutes at 3500F.

Curried Rice 'n Chicken Bake

Servings: 3
Cooking Time: 45 Minutes

Ingredients:

- 1 clove garlic, minced
- 6 ounces skinless, boneless chicken breast halves - cut into 1-inch cubes
- 1/2 cup water
- 1/2 (8 ounce) can stewed tomatoes
- 1-1/2 teaspoons lemon juice
- 1-1/2 teaspoons curry powder
- 1/2 cube chicken bouillon
- 1/2 bay leaf (optional)
- 1/4 cup and 2 tablespoons quick-cooking brown rice
- 1/4 cup raisins
- 1/4 teaspoon ground cinnamon
- 1/8 teaspoon salt

Directions:

1. Lightly grease baking pan of Air Fryer with cooking spray.
2. Stir in bay leaf, garlic, salt, cinnamon, bouillon, curry powder, lemon juice, raisins, brown rice, stewed tomatoes, and water. For minutes, cook on 360oF. Halfway through cooking time, stir in chicken and mix well.
3. Cover pan with foil.
4. Cook for 15 minutes at 390oF, remove foil, cook for 10 minutes until tops are lightly browned.
5. Serve and enjoy.

Tea Glazed Chicken Recipe

Servings: 6
Cooking Time: 40 Minutes

Ingredients:

- 6 chicken legs
- 6 black tea bags
- 1/4 tsp. red pepper flakes
- 1 tbsp. olive oil
- 1/2 cup pineapple preserves
- 1/2 cup apricot preserves
- 1 cup hot water
- 1 tbsp. soy sauce
- 1 onion; chopped
- Salt and black pepper to the taste

Directions:

1. Put the hot water in a bowl, add tea bags, leave aside covered for minutes; discard bags at the end and transfer tea to another bowl.
2. Add soy sauce, pepper flakes, apricot and pineapple preserves, whisk really well and take off heat.
3. Season chicken with salt and pepper, rub with oil, put in your Air Fryer and cook at 0 °F, for 5 minutes.
4. Spread onion on the bottom of a baking dish that fits your Air Fryer, add chicken pieces, drizzle the tea glaze on top, introduce in your Air Fryer and cook at 320 °F, for 25 minutes. Divide everything on plates and serve.

Turkey And Lime Gravy

Servings: 4
Cooking Time: 25 Minutes

Ingredients:

- 1 big turkey breast, skinless, boneless, cubed and browned
- Juice of 1 lime
- Zest of 1 lime, grated
- 1 cup chicken stock
- 3 tablespoons parsley, chopped
- 4 tablespoons butter, melted
- 2 tablespoons thyme, chopped
- A pinch of salt and black pepper

Directions:

1. Heat up a pan that fits the Air Fryer with the butter over medium heat, add all the ingredients except the turkey, whisk, bring to a simmer and cook for 5 minutes.
2. Add the turkey cubes, put the pan in the Air Fryer and cook at 380 degrees F for 20 minutes.
3. Divide the meat between plates, drizzle the gravy all over and serve.

Gourmet Chicken Omelet

Servings: 2
Cooking Time: 15 Minutes

Ingredients:

- 4 eggs, whisked
- 4 oz. ground chicken
- ½ cup scallions, finely chopped
- 2 cloves garlic, finely minced
- ½ tsp. salt
- ½ tsp. ground black pepper
- ½ tsp. paprika
- 1 tsp. dried thyme
- Dash of hot sauce

Directions:

1. Mix together all the ingredients in a bowl, ensuring to incorporate everything well.
2. Lightly grease two oven-safe ramekins with vegetable oil. Divide the mixture between them.
3. Transfer them to the Air Fryer, and air fry at 0°F for 13 minutes.
4. Ensure they are cooked through and serve immediately.

Chicken Fry Recipe From The Mediterranean

Servings: 2
Cooking Time: 21 Minutes

Ingredients:

- 2 boneless skinless chicken breast halves (6 ounces each)
- 3 tablespoons olive oil
- 6 pitted Greek or ripe olives, sliced
- 2 tablespoons capers, drained
- 1/2-pint grape tomatoes
- 1/4 teaspoon salt
- 1/4 teaspoon pepper

Directions:

1. Lightly grease baking pan of Air Fryer with cooking spray.
2. Add chicken and season with pepper and salt.
3. Brown for minutes per side in preheated 390 o F Air Fryer.
4. Stir in capers, olives, tomatoes, and oil.
5. Cook for 1minutes at 330oF.
6. Serve and enjoy.

Old-Fashioned Chicken Drumettes

Servings: 3
Cooking Time: 30 Minutes

Ingredients:

- 1/3 cup all-purpose flour
- 1/2 teaspoon ground white pepper
- 1 teaspoon seasoning salt
- 1 teaspoon garlic paste
- 1 teaspoon rosemary
- 1 whole egg + 1 egg white
- 6 chicken drumettes
- 1 heaping tablespoon fresh chives, chopped

Directions:

1. Start by preheating your Air Fryer to 390 degrees.
2. Mix the flour with white pepper, salt, garlic paste, and rosemary in a small-sized bowl.
3. In another bowl, beat the eggs until frothy.
4. Dip the chicken into the flour mixture, then into the beaten eggs; coat with the flour mixture one more time.
5. Cook the chicken drumettes for 22 minutes. Serve warm, garnished with chives.

Onion And Cayenne Chicken Tenders

Servings: 2
Cooking Time: 10 Minutes

Ingredients:

- 8 oz chicken fillet
- 1 teaspoon minced onion
- ¼ teaspoon onion powder
- ¼ teaspoon salt
- ½ teaspoon cayenne pepper
- Cooking spray

Directions:

1. Cut the chicken fillet on 2 tenders and sprinkle with salt, onion powder, and cayenne pepper.
2. Then preheat the Air Fryer to 365F.
3. Spray the Air Fryer basket with cooking spray from inside and place the chicken tenders in it. Top the chicken with minced onion and cook for minutes at 365F.

Quick 'n Easy Brekky Eggs 'n Cream

Servings: 2
Cooking Time: 15 Minutes

Ingredients:

- 2 eggs
- 2 tablespoons coconut cream
- A dash of Spanish paprika
- Salt and pepper to taste

Directions:

1. Preheat the Air Fryer for 5 minutes.
2. Place the eggs and coconut cream in a bowl. Season with salt and pepper to taste then whisk until fluffy.
3. Pour into greased ramekins and sprinkle with Spanish paprika.
4. Place in the Air Fryer.
5. Bake for 1minutes at 3500F.

Loaded Chicken Burgers

Servings: 5
Cooking Time: 30 Minutes

Ingredients:

- 2 tablespoons olive oil
- 1 onion, finely chopped
- 2 green garlic, chopped
- 6 ounces mushrooms, chopped
- 1 ½ pounds ground chicken
- 1/3 cup parmesan cheese
- 1/4 cup pork rinds, crushed
- 1 tablespoon fish sauce
- 1 tablespoon tamari sauce
- 1 teaspoon Dijon mustard
- 5 soft hamburger buns
- 5 lettuce leaves

Directions:

1. Heat a nonstick skillet over medium-high heat; add olive oil. Once hot, sauté the onion until tender and translucent, about 3 minutes.
2. Add the garlic and mushrooms and cook an additional minutes, stirring frequently.
3. Add the ground chicken, cheese, pork rind, fish sauce, and tamari sauce; mix until everything is well incorporated.
4. Form the mixture into 5 patties. Transfer the patties to the lightly greased cooking basket.
5. Cook in the preheated Air Fryer at 370 degrees F for 8 minutes; then, flip them over and cook for 8 minutes on the other side.
6. Serve on burger buns, garnished with mustard and lettuce. Bon appétit!

Flavorful Cornish Hen

Servings: 3
Cooking Time: 25 Minutes

Ingredients:

- 1 Cornish hen, wash and pat dry
- 1 tbsp olive oil
- 1 tsp smoked paprika
- 1/2 tsp garlic powder
- Pepper
- Salt

Directions:

1. Coat Cornish hen with olive oil and rub with paprika, garlic powder, pepper, and salt.
2. Place Cornish hen in the Air Fryer basket.
3. Cook at 0 F for 25 minutes. Turn halfway through.
4. Slice and serve.

Sweet Turmeric Chicken Wings

Servings: 8
Cooking Time: 15 Minutes

Ingredients:

- 8 chicken wings
- 1 teaspoon Splenda
- 1 teaspoon ground turmeric
- ½ teaspoon cayenne pepper
- 1 tablespoon avocado oil

Directions:

1. Mix up Splenda and avocado oil and stir the mixture until Splenda is dissolved.
2. Then rub the chicken wings with ground turmeric and cayenne pepper.
3. Brush the chicken wings with sweet avocado oil from both sides.
4. Preheat the Air Fryer to 390F. Place the chicken wings in the Air Fryer and cook them for minutes.

Bbq Chicken Recipe From Greece

Servings: 4
Cooking Time: 24 Minutes

Ingredients:

- 1 (8 ounce) container fat-free plain yogurt
- 2 tablespoons fresh lemon juice
- 2 teaspoons dried oregano
- 1-pound skinless, boneless chicken breast halves - cut into 1-inch pieces
- 1 large red onion, cut into wedges
- 1/2 teaspoon lemon zest
- 1/2 teaspoon salt
- 1 large green bell pepper, cut into 1 1/2-inch pieces
- 1/3 cup crumbled feta cheese with basil and sun-dried tomatoes
- 1/4 teaspoon ground black pepper
- 1/4 teaspoon crushed dried rosemary

Directions:

1. In a shallow dish, mix well rosemary, pepper, salt, oregano, lemon juice, lemon zest, feta cheese, and yogurt. Add chicken and toss well to coat. Marinate in the ref for 3 hours.
2. Thread bell pepper, onion, and chicken pieces in skewers. Place on skewer rack.
3. For 12 minutes, cook on 0oF. Halfway through cooking time, turnover skewers. If needed, cook in batches.
4. Serve and enjoy.

Grilled Oregano Chicken

Servings: 6
Cooking Time: 40 Minutes

Ingredients:

- 3 pounds chicken breasts
- 2 tablespoons oregano, chopped
- 4 cloves of garlic, minced
- 1 tablespoon grated lemon zest
- 2 tablespoons fresh lemon juice
- Salt and pepper to taste

Directions:

1. Preheat the Air Fryer at 3750F.
2. Place the grill pan accessory in the Air Fryer.
3. Season the chicken with oregano, garlic, lemon zest, lemon juice, salt and pepper.
4. Grill for minutes and flip every 10 minutes to cook evenly.

Cayenne And Turmeric Chicken Strips

Servings: 6
Cooking Time: 14 Minutes

Ingredients:

- 2-pound chicken breast, skinless, boneless
- 1 teaspoon salt
- 1 teaspoon ground turmeric
- ½ teaspoon cayenne pepper
- 1 egg, beaten
- 2 tablespoons coconut flour

Directions:

1. Cut the chicken breast into the strips and sprinkle with salt, ground turmeric, and cayenne pepper.
2. Then add beaten egg in the chicken strips and stir the mixture.
3. After this, add coconut flour and stir it.
4. Preheat the Air Fryer to 400F.
5. Put ½ part of all chicken strips in the Air Fryer basket in one layer and cook them for 7 minutes.
6. Repeat the same steps with the remaining chicken strips.

Green Curry Hot Chicken Drumsticks

Servings: 4

Cooking Time: 25 Minutes

Ingredients:

- 2 tbsp green curry paste
- 3 tbsp coconut cream
- Salt and black pepper
- ½ fresh jalapeno chili, finely chopped
- A handful of fresh parsley, roughly chopped

Directions:

1. In a bowl, add drumsticks, paste, cream, salt, black pepper and jalapeno; coat the chicken well.
2. Arrange the drumsticks in the Air Fryer and cook for 6 minutes at 400 F, flipping once halfway through. Serve with fresh cilantro.

Breaded Chicken Tenderloins

Servings: 4
Cooking Time: 12 Minutes

Ingredients:

- 1 egg, beaten
- ½ cup breadcrumbs
- 8 skinless, boneless chicken tenderloins
- 2 tablespoons vegetable oil

Directions:

1. Preheat the Air Fryer to 355 o F and grease an Air Fryer basket.
2. Whisk the egg in a bowl and mix vegetable oil and breadcrumbs in another bowl.
3. Dip the chicken tenderloins into the whisked egg and then coat with the breadcrumb mixture.
4. Arrange the chicken tenderloins into the Air Fryer basket and cook for about 12 minutes.
5. Dish out the chicken tenderloins into a platter and serve hot.

Chestnuts 'n Mushroom Chicken Casserole

Servings: 2
Cooking Time: 35 Minutes

Ingredients:

- 1 (10.75 ounce) can condensed cream of chicken soup
- 1 (4.5 ounce) can mushrooms, drained
- 1 1/2 teaspoons melted butter
- 1 cup shredded, cooked chicken meat
- 1/2 (8 ounce) can water chestnuts, drained (optional)
- 1/2 cup mayonnaise
- 1/2 teaspoon lemon juice
- 1/4 cup shredded Cheddar cheese
- 1/8 teaspoon curry powder
- 1-1/4 cups cooked chopped broccoli

Directions:

1. Lightly grease baking pan of Air Fryer with cooking spray.
2. Evenly spread broccoli on bottom of pan. Sprinkle chicken on top, followed by water chestnuts and mushrooms.
3. In a bowl, whisk well melted butter, curry powder, lemon juice, mayonnaise, and soup. Pour over chicken mixture in pan. Cover pan with foil.
4. For 25 minutes, cook on 360oF.
5. Remove foil from pan and cook for another 10 minutes or until top is a golden brown.
6. Serve and enjoy.

Must-Serve Turkey Breasts With Parsley

Servings: 2
Cooking Time: 25 Minutes + Marinating Time

Ingredients:

- 1/2 tablespoon minced fresh parsley
- 1 ½ tablespoons Worcestershire sauce
- Sea salt flakes and cracked black peppercorns, to savor
- 1 ½ tablespoons olive oil
- 1/3 turkey breasts, halved
- 1 ½ tablespoons rice vinegar
- 1/2 teaspoon marjoram

Directions:

1. Set the Air Fryer to cook at 395 degrees. In a bowl, mix all ingredients together; make sure to coat turkey breast well.
2. Set aside to marinate for at least 3 hours.
3. Roast each turkey piece for 2minutes; make sure to pause the machine and flip once to roast evenly. Bon appétit!

Special Maple-Glazed Chicken

Servings: 4
Cooking Time: 20 Minutes

Ingredients:

- 2 ½ tbsp. maple syrup
- 1 tbsp. tamari soy sauce
- 1 tbsp. oyster sauce
- 1 tsp. fresh lemon juice
- 1 tsp. minced fresh ginger
- 1 tsp. garlic puree
- Seasoned salt and freshly ground pepper, to taste
- 2 boneless, skinless chicken breasts

Directions:

1. In a bowl, combine the maple syrup, tamari sauce, oyster sauce, lemon juice, fresh ginger and garlic puree. This is your marinade.
2. Sprinkle the chicken breasts with salt and pepper.
3. Coat the chicken breasts with the marinade. Place some foil over the bowl and refrigerate for hours, or overnight if possible.
4. Remove the chicken from the marinade. Place it in the Air Fryer and fry for 15 minutes at 365°F, flipping each one once or twice throughout.
5. In the meantime, add the remaining marinade to a pan over medium heat. Allow the marinade to simmer for 3 - minutes until it has reduced by half.
6. Pour over the cooked chicken and serve.